Detroit's Near Eastsiders

A journey of Excellence Against The Odds
1920's - 1960's

Detroit's Near Eastsiders... A Journey of Excellence Against The Odds: 1920's - 1960's

ISBN 978-1-888754-07-0

Library of Congress Control Number: 2008922228

The Near Eastsiders
18301 W. 13 Mile Road #A4N
Southfield, MI 48076
Telephone 248-593-8322

Era Williamson — *Chairperson*
Lenore Lewis Evans — *Vice-Chairperson*
Joynal Muthleb — *Treasurer*
Sylvia Muthleb — *Correspondence Secretary*

Founding Members
William Edmonson
Dr. Robert Ellison
Eugene Elzy
John Henry
Teola Hunter
John Kline, Ph.D.
Ernest Wagner

Justine Wylie — *Editor-in-Chief & Writer*
Council Cargle — *Editor*

Book Producer / Layout Editor: Herbert Metoyer, Cane River Media
Cover Design: Herbert Metoyer, Cane River Media
Published by: The Detroit Black Writer's Guild for The Near Eastsiders

The Near Eastsiders is a non-profit literary group. Their goal is to preserve and present in literary form, the historic significance of the collective contributions of African-Americans who not only survived, but thrived during a turbulent period in history.

Printed in the United States of America

DEDICATION

The Near Eastsiders dedicate this book, *A Journey of Excellence Against the Odds,* to the migrants of the past, the participants of the present and the beneficiaries of the future.

Georgette and Sidney Lewis

INTRODUCTION

On the Near Eastside of Detroit, the years (1920-1960) were a time of hope for blacks as they began their *"Journey of excellence Against the Odds."* It seems fitting that this book telling of those blacks who not only survived, but thrived should be written and presented to you by a group of people who themselves lived in this area, at these times, and who converged to lend their diverse talents, their unique perspectives, and yes, their passions to tell their truths through their writings, their memoirs and their collective memories, a story that needs to be told.

Our story cannot be appreciated without understanding the history of racism in Detroit. According to the 1920 U.S. Census records, the black population of Detroit was 40,000. Most were from the rural South. Here we were relegated to the oldest, shabbiest and most overcrowded parts of the city. We were excluded from most hotels, restaurants and other public places. This was a time when most of the teachers were white, most heroes were white and the fairy tale characters were white. Those of us lucky enough to be employed worked primarily as unskilled laborers and in custodial work. Some had good paying jobs in the automobile and related industries. A number of us worked as porters and redcaps. Others were the entrepreneurs and the professionally trained. The black middle class, the working poor and the unemployed all struggled to survive. But we were and are a remarkable people. It sometimes seemed that we could take the biblical seven loaves of bread and a few fish and feed the multitudes that were our nuclear and extended families.

By 1960, The Near Eastside had undergone a dramatic change. As they prospered, many black Detroiters moved from the Near Eastside to other areas of the city and to the northern suburbs. A modern day Goliath, I-75, the Chrysler Freeway, replaced the Hastings Street corridor. This freeway was merciless. In the name of progress, it decimated homes, scattered families and forced the relocation or abandonment of scores of businesses. Hastings Street became a part of our collective memory and modern day folklore.

We *say*, "I remember" or "Remember when?" But memory cheats us, trivializing and minimizing the pain and passions of those years. This is why it is so important that the significance of these collective memories be chronicled. It is imperative that those of us who remember and who lived the struggle in our journey for excellence against the odds, record for posterity, the experiences of the people and the events and places that have played a major part in the development of the Near Eastside.

The Near Eastsiders are proud to have taken this opportunity to travel back in time and to research and recreate their history for future generations. We invite you to journey with us into the heart of the Near Eastside in *our* stream of time. We promise you will savor this experience.

Justine Rogers Wylie

TABLE OF CONTENTS

ACKNOWLEDGEMENTS

The Near Eastsiders wish to acknowledge and to thank:

The Pastorate of Bethel A.M.E. Church who so kindly contributed without recompense, the use of the church's resources for our many meetings throughout the years. There are very few Near Eeastsiders who have not been the recipient of growth experiences through teachings and activities at Bethel A.M.E. Bethel has been the spiritual home of many of the Near Eastsiders. The church's hosting of the Near Eastsiders is but one example of Bethel's continuing service to the community.

Attorney and Mrs. Myzell Sowell for their generous monetary contribution to the Near Eastsiders for the publication of this book. Their contribution lifted our spirits. We felt encouraged to know that someone of significance considered our mission worthy of monetary support.

If a picture is indeed worth a thousand words, then we are truly indebted to **Orlin Jones** who graciously granted the Near Eastsiders access to his magnificent collection of pictures, photos and memorabilia.

Jean Everage, a Near Eastsider, whose concern for the publication of this book, at times, took precedent over her very real health concerns as she researched and recovered photos that have enriched this book.

Walter P.Reuther Library, Wayne State University

A special thank you to **Dr. Norman McCray** and **Suesetta Talbert McCree** who have successfully traveled the road to publication earlier. They have the insight that only comes from experience. Both have been uncommonly generous and supportive, sharing information and ideas and lending encouragement to the Near Eastsiders as we embarked on our **"Journey."**

Valaida Benson, a near eastsider for the script and orchestration of Hastings Street Revisited that made out first fundraiser a success.

Many people have helped in the completion of this book, but none more than **Herbert Metoyer, Publisher** who has read, reacted, advised, edited, designed, and prepared this book for publication. Metoyer did with aplomb whatever he knew was needed to bring our **"Journey"** to fruition. He continues to bring Detroit's Black History into prominence through The Detroit Black Writers' Guild and his Cane River Media Publishing Company.

CHAPTER ONE
WELCOME TO OUR WORLD

An Insiders View of the Near Eastside

Throw open the pages of this book and step into decades past in dynamic Detroit. All of those who were privileged to have lived in Detroit, and especially those who lived on the Near Eastside in this era will find themselves transported into a past they will remember with nostalgia and with joy.

Detroit was not a perfect city but it had all of the elements that combined to make a city and a community great. The times were challenging, and African-Americans living in Detroit rose to meet these challenges. Long before Detroit's first black Mayor, Coleman Alexander Young emerged to lead the city beyond the Civil Rights era. Before Berry Gordy and his Motown put Detroit at the top of the world's musical charts, the Near Eastside was the hub of African-American life in this city.

The uninitiated may ask, "What is this 'Near Eastside' that you speak of?" The geographic boundaries were East Grand Boulevard on the north, Adams Street on the south, Russell Street on the east and Woodward Avenue on the west. The Near Eastside was only a small part of what grew to become the nation's 5th largest city, yet its impact was mighty.

Picture, courtesy of The Heritage House Museum

1

The Near Eastside was the place where most black people lived, separated from most whites. The Near Eastside has been described as a tough part of a tough town, although many of its inhabitants did not share this appraisal. The inhabitants were primarily black people and their descendants who had migrated from the rural south seeking jobs and an economic toehold in a newly industrialized America. We say primarily because European immigrants, Jewish people, Chaldeans, southern whites and Caribbean Islanders all shared the Near Eastside, making it, for a time, the most integrated part of Detroit.

What made the struggle for a decent living more difficult was the fact that southern whites were pouring into Detroit with the same goals and needs. These whites came with their families and their same values that included a strong belief in segregation of the races. Segregationist practices relegated black people to a defined part of Detroit, primarily the Near Eastside.

While many maligned the Near Eastside, its isolation from much of white commerce worked to its advantage in many ways. Hundreds of black businesses sprang up. This plethora of businesses and businessmen was awesome in its ability to provide anything a black person needed. It didn't matter whether one needed a shoeshine or a tailor, fresh fruit or fresh flowers, an oral surgeon or an attorney. Everything was available on the Near Eastside. The money made on the Near Eastside allowed many black families to move to the Westside and to the North End. This was the launching place where many of the entrepreneurs went on to fame and fortune.

This black community was actually a city within a city, linked by race and religious faith, by love of family and by the belief that they could and would provide for their children, something that most of them never had. Many blacks had little formal education, some had attended high school, and a very few were college educated. They all understood the value of a good education. Out of

Many Blacks migrrated to the Detroit area seeking employment in the auto industry.

Detroit Labor Day Parade, September, 1959 -
Jean Everage, seated on left, with three co-workers of AT&T Telephone Operators. Lyndon B. Johnson,
Democratic presidential hopeful, spoke at this Labor Day Parade.

Ralph Johnson Bunche

this Near Eastside came the actors, the athletes, attorneys, physicians, firemen, teachers, nurses, musicians and entrepreneurs who have formed the backbone of life in Detroit.

Out of this Near Eastside came **Ralph Johnson Bunche,** the first African-American Nobel Peace Prize recipient. He was born on August 7, 1903, at 434 Anthony Street in Detroit Michigan, the son of a barber and the grandson of a slave.

The best times of Bunche's childhood are recorded in a letter Bunche wrote in late 1959 to William T. Nobel of the Detroit News and cited in Brian Urguhart's work, *Ralph Bunche.* He recalled that he enjoyed:

…"hitching up my sled in winter onto the tailgates of horse-drawn beer trucks, swimming on Belle Isle in the summer and in the river down by the firehouse…the thrill of the circus parades, and particularly the calliope at the end of it, when Barnum and Bailey came to town and the still bigger thrill of slipping into the big tent under the canvas

sides; rooting for the Tigers and especially Ty Cobb; Hawking newspapers on the street and how we yelled; and the excitement when "extras" came out as they frequently did then and never do now."

———

When Charles Dickens wrote in his *Tale of Two Cities*, "It was the best of times, it was the worst of times," his description of those times could be said to mirror that of Detroit in the years spanning 1920-1960. This city, this world and this nation were embroiled in major changes, in turbulence and triumphs that historians would record for posterity. Although this book is about Detroit and Detroiters, our city did not exist in a vacuum. Detroit was affected not only by world events, but also by the social, political, economic and racial climate that existed in the United States of America during this period.

In 1920, the right to vote was extended to women in our country. Women of all colors began to exercise and to extend their newly found freedom. Jazz was an outlet for rebellion and dances such as the *Charleston, Fox Trot and The Big Apple* reflected that rebellion. Duke Ellington, Louis Armstrong and blues singer, Bessie Smith and Lil Green were some of the musicians who reflected the times in their music. Women who may have sung hymns at home began to sing the blues. Lipstick and makeup that once had been the province of entertainers and "sporting women" became commonplace in the neighborhoods. So-called *Black and Tan* cabarets began to emerge in the largely segregated entertainment area that became known as Paradise Valley.

This was the period that saw the end of Prohibition. Detroit was a major player in the illegal sale of liquor. The Detroit River is said to have been the gateway for the largest importation of Black Market liquor in the U.S.A. The flow of liquor through the newly built Detroit/Windsor Tunnel was so enormous that it was dubbed The Detroit/Windsor Funnel. Detroit had its own criminal Mafia, the so-called "Purple Gang," a Jewish group that controlled the illegal sale and importation of liquor in Detroit. This "Purple Gang" was so powerful that it allegedly challenged Al Capone's Chicago crime family for dominance in Black Market liquor distribution.

Among the most significant events was the stock market crash of 1929 that impoverished black and white Americans, not equally, but alike. As the saying goes, "When white America sneezes, black America gets pneumonia." This is perhaps an overstatement, for in truth, October, 1929 began a period of great privation for most Americans. According to the 1930 U.S. Census, the average wage for U.S. workers was $1,288. By 1932, the average wage for U.S. workers had dropped to $843.

Many people had come to Detroit, primarily from the rural south, to work in the auto industry, which was paying their employees higher wages than they had previously earned. When the stock market crashed, thousands of Detroiters lost their jobs. Workers were laid off; others were fired outright. Without jobs, many of the unemployed were unable to pay their bills or to obtain credit. It is difficult to envision today, but there are old time Detroiters alive today who remember when *"Bread Lines" and "Soup Lines"* were extremely important to the thousands of Detroiters who were struggling to survive. Some of them remember witnessing the demonstrations by hungry and angry Detroit citizens in front of City Hall when the City of Detroit went broke and they issued script in place of money to city workers.

The migration of southerners to Detroit did not stop when the economy was brought to its knees by *The Great Depression.* Families continued to move to the Detroit area. The expectation, the hope of escaping oppressive racist practices was incentive enough for many blacks to move north. In Detroit, many found families, friends, a community that understood the migrants' needs, their goals, and respected them for it.

Families shared homes and apartments with relatives and strangers in an effort to survive. A communal spirit was born of this struggle to survive that in retrospect, seems remarkable. Out of the shared needs, the shared culture and the shared religion, black Americans came together and prepared for the better times that were ahead.

Children going to Green Pastures Camp, (circa 1940's)

Hope, prayers and determination were perhaps the only thing that black Americans had in abundance. With widespread poverty and the inability to fully experience the American dream, black entrepreneurs stepped up to the plate and took their place in Detroit's business arena. Some found assistance from the Booker T. Washington Trade Association whose primary purpose was to assist black businesses in this time of economic privation.

Many of these businesses were small, primarily mom and pop businesses. Most of them bought on credit and sold on credit. When the Fred A. Anderson Funeral Home on Willis between St. Antoine and Beaubien, gave bags of candy and fruit to children at Christmas time, the lines of children would extend around the corner. Small grocery store owners would save scraps of leftover meat for the neighborhood dogs. The Eastern Market at Russell and Mack extending to Riopelle on the east and Gratiot Avenue on the south was a place where one could find fresh fruits and vegetables for little or sometimes *no* money; where at

Mrs. Julia Everage, Jean Everage & Teola Cranon on Medbury Park

Playground at Brewster Homes, Detroit, Michigan, August 1946.

6

Reverend William H. Peck, Powerbroker

Neighborhood movie theaters lured moviegoers in with the promise of free dishes. The *Goodfellows,* a philanthropic organization, were a welcome intrusion in the neighborhoods when they came during the Christmas season bearing gifts of toys and clothing.

Before the booming industrialization of World War II opened up many and varied job opportunities for black men and women, religious leaders as The Reverend Robert Bradby of Second Baptist, The Reverend William H. Peck of Bethel A.M.E. and the Reverend Horace White of Plymouth Congregational Church were the major powerbrokers in the provision of employment for black families who had migrated to the Detroit area. These men of the cloth, through their relationships with Henry Ford and the Ford Motor Company, could guarantee a job in the auto industry to any job seeker recommended by them, albeit many of the jobs were in the Ford Rouge Foundry or in production lines. Only rarely did blacks obtain the better paying assembly lines jobs

_____.

closing time, bruised fruit or vegetables left on the ground or in abandoned crates were free for the taking.

An automotive assembly line depicting Black & White employees working together.

The Edmonson Family Supporting The War Effort

Betty Edmonson

William Edmonson

John Edmonson

David Edmonson

World War II

A Tuskegee Airman over France. Margo was piloted by Ltc. Alexander Jefferson of Detroit. (Drawing by Herb Metoyer)

When World War Two began in Europe, the United States began to gear up for the war that was to be thrust upon Americans by the Japanese attack on Pearl Harbor in Hawaii. A wind of change was in the air that brought anxiety and apprehension to Americans.

Selective Service began to register men for the draft. The Michigan National Guard was mobilized for active duty. In the neighborhoods, there was talk of war. Families became frightened at the thought that their fathers, husbands, sons, uncles and cousins might be compelled to go to war. There was fear that war would come to America and that bombs would be dropped on our cities. Air-Raid Wardens were selected for each block in the city. There were air-raid drills and trial blackouts. School children practiced hiding under their desks in case of an air raid. Songs of war and patriotism dominated the airwaves. Nat King Cole sang one of the war's popular theme songs, a song that said in part, " Don't talk too much. Don't be too hip, cause the slip of a lip might sink a ship." Americans were truly apprehensive despite remembering the words of President Roosevelt who, seeking to assuage the fears generated during the Great Depression asserted, "There is nothing to fear but fear itself."

In December 1941 when the United States officially entered the war, all automobile production came to a halt. Automobile factories became a major part of the war effort. Detroit was transformed into the "Arsenal of Democracy." The migration to Detroit that had slowed because of the sagging economy began again full force. The promise of high wages in the new war factories lured many thousands of migrants from the rural south. These migrants came with high hopes and expectations as well as their prejudices. There was a large gap between hope and reality. Few found the proverbial *Promised Land*.

In the factories, there were 48-hour workweeks that put a surplus of money in workers' pockets but few places to spend it. Meats, butter and oils, sugar, coffee and gasoline were among the things rationed. Many people became regular commuters to Canada to buy the meat and sugar rationed in the U.S.A. Perhaps the most crucial shortage was found in the housing market and in the intolerances that the white southerners brought with them.

For the first time, women were a major part of the work force. These women drove streetcars and buses and worked at the many industrial jobs that opened up. Many young women joined the armed services or volunteered with the USO. The women were making more money than they had in the past, but outlets for spending were fewer. Many consumer goods were in short supply. Automobile production was at a halt; gasoline was rationed, as were many big-ticket items. There were relatively few men around as many were in the military. This left many women with time on their hands, money in their pockets and a diminished ability to exercise their adult options.

―――――

Julia Lee Carter (*USO Hostess, World War II*)

Pfc Sidney Lewis

Salather Pierce (Philippine Islands, 1947)

Women Recall Wartime Jobs and Bias

DETROIT FREE PRESS
BY REBECCA BEACH Sunday, **March** 9, **1986**
Free Press Staff Writer

As able-bodied men were called to war in 1942, women left their homes and stepped into men's jobs, such as operating Detroit's streetcar network. The third annual meeting of the Conductorettes and Motorettes of World War II was Saturday, and 12 women, many in their 70's gathered to talk about the city and their old jobs.

In December 1942, Pauline Taylor, age 31, took the Detroit civil service examination and was given a job as conductorette. She and 324 other women were hired to operate the streetcars, and although their jobs lasted only until July 1946, the memories are fresh.

Taylor still has the citation she received for saving a motorman's life by pleading with an angry mob during the riot of 1943. "These were the same people he'd given free rides to, his friends," she said.

Memories of the riot, V-J Day, making 96 cents **an** hour, the polite riders — and annoying ones — from the auto plants bring laughter and memories of younger days. Taylor remembered the Oakland line, dubbed "the fish line" because of the fish stores that lined the route. She remembered the motorman who always stopped at his girlfriend's house to pick up a sack lunch. And she recalled being fired July 24, 1946.

"WE FELT PATRIOTIC working for the war effort," said Maryanne Thompkins, 65. "We thought we'd have those jobs until the men came back. Then they fired us and started hiring people (men) off the street."

The women picketed city hall. Joining them on the picket lines were the Detroit Consumers League, the National Women's Party, the Business and Professional Women's Club, the NAACP and the Women Lawyers Association, led by Martha Griffiths, now lieutenant governor of Michigan and then chair of the Detroit Women's Committee to Fight Sex Discrimination. "She volunteered to fight for us," said Thompkins. "She was a scrapper."

The women lost their bid to get their jobs back. When many reapplied to the city, they were told that the recruiting standards had changed and the civil service examinations were for jobs to be held exclusively by men.

"Their minds were made up," said Polk, whose son Robert Polk now heads the Detroit Department of Transportation.

The motorettes and conductorettes went back to homes and families and on to other jobs. "But the situation wasn't that bad," said Polk. "You could get a job anywhere."

Maryanne Thompkins (Conductress)
(1943 Photo)

City of Detroit Street Car, Michigan Avenue (April 2, 1920).

BUY

US WAR

BONDS

Above, Thompkins and a few of her friends: Back row from left, Talu Massey. Adlee Bell and Mary Scarber; center row, Agnes Foust, Lucille Miller Foster, Mary Hicks, Pauline Taylor and Josephine Polk; front row, Thompkins, Ellen Ferguson and Jane Ravarra.

VETERANS REMEMBER
During World War II, black soldiers battled
racism in the ranks as well as the enemy abroad

FIGHT ON TWO FRONTS

Essie Woods spent her childhood between a small home in Augusta, GA and a castle on the Hudson River in upstate New York. Thanks to parents who worked as a butler and a maid for a rich family who summered in New York and wintered down South, she got used to travel early.

That might have helped her later when she became a member of the Women's Army Corps 6888th Central Postal Directory Battalion, the first Black women to be sent overseas. The Six Triple Eight, a unit of more than 800 Black women, subsequently broke all records for redirecting mail to

nearly 7 million U.S. Troops and personnel in Europe during World War II.

The women worked in stuffy former schools, in three 8-hour shifts, 24 hours a day, sitting at tables piled high with mail, sifting and sorting, to make sure war-weary soldiers heard from home.

"Our job was to get the mail to the front," said Woods, who was 88 at the time this article appeared in the Free Press. "It was backlogged because the fellows had not been able to keep up with it... We had three shifts and then on top of that, they had those bombs going off around us.... But we were lucky."

13

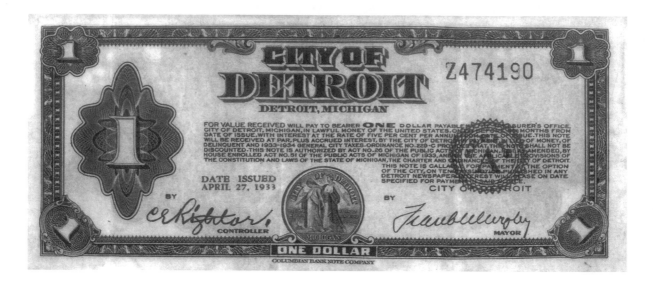

During the war, several measures were taken to keep the economy afloat. Above is a copy the script issued by the City of Detroit. Script was used in place of money.

Below is a copy of a War Ration book containing stamps that were used to purchase your allotment of high demand items and groceries.

4

№ 108676 EH

UNITED STATES OF AMERICA
OFFICE OF PRICE ADMINISTRATION

WAR RATION BOOK FOUR

Issued to *Rosalind J. Sandler*
(Print first, middle, and last names)

Complete address *218 Forest St.*

Marshall, Michigan

READ BEFORE SIGNING

In accepting this book, I recognize that it remains the property of the United States Government. I will use it only in the manner and for the purposes authorized by the Office of Price Administration.

Void if Altered

(Signature)

It is a criminal offense to violate rationing regulations.

OPA Form R-145   16—35570-1

AFC. 2001/001/2671

| 52 COFFEE | 72 SPARE | 71 SPARE | 40 SUGAR |

Marcus Burden

Eugene Hill (Circa 1951 - 1953)

Sgt. Marvin Wayne Rogers

Samuel Carter & Army Friend

Woods spent a year overseas and encountered rampant racism in a segregated army. "But," she said, "it didn't affect our work because we were determined to prove we could handle the situation, and it would have been a reflection on our race if we had not made good."

———

— 1943 Riot —

The housing supply was insufficient for the many migrants who flooded Detroit. The Brewster Homes or so-called projects were the only public housing that existed for blacks at the start of the war. Blacks were paying higher rent than were whites for inferior accommodations. Blacks were discriminated in public accommodations and in the military. Many whites were resentful of blacks who worked with them on the production and assembly lines. Many racially tinged incidents, verbal and physical, were precursors to the riot that occurred on June 20, 1943. Following the melees that ensued when blacks were finally allowed to move into the Sojourner Truth projects in 1942, racial tensions in Detroit were near the boiling point.

On that memorable Sunday at Belle Isle Park, rumor spread in the black community that white men had thrown a black woman and her baby off of the Belle Isle Bridge. Another rumor sweeping the white neighborhoods was that black men had raped and murdered a white woman on the Belle Isle Bridge. Although neither rumor was ever substantiated, the repercussions from that June 20th incident remained for many years to come. The outbreak was so severe that President Roosevelt ordered federal troops in armored cars and automatic weapons to cool the rebellion. The riot lasted 36 hours and claimed 34 lives, 25 of them black. More than 1800 citizens were arrested for looting and other violations.

When the riot was over, a walk down Hastings Street was revealing. From Canfield to Medbury, not one white business had been left intact by looters and rioters. One Near Eastsider recounts that in the aftermath of the riot, a visit to McFall's Funeral Home on the corner of Canfield and Hastings revealed eight bodies in the mortuary rather than the usual one or two. Reportedly, these were victims of the riot.

The year following the riot marked the beginning of *"white flight"* from some of the

Our Old Neighborhood. On-lookers surveying the damage after the 1943 riot.

Young Negro (extreme right) makes dash across Woodward Avenue, Detroit, with a mob of whites in pursuit. Many riot victims who wound up in hospitals didn't know what it was all about. A Detroit news reporter found a white man and a Negro sitting side by side at one hospital, waiting for treatment. The white man said he was coming home from work at an aircraft plant; when he got off the streetcar, a gang beat him up. The Negro said some men started chasing him and he tore his hand on a barbed-wire fence getting away. Both were utterly bewildered.

Negro owned car blazes on Detroit Street after it was overturned and set afire by mob. Scores of automobiles, from flashy Lincolns to shabby flivvers, were destroyed during the riot. Once the mob pulled a Negro from his car and beat him in front of his wife and small daughter. So many stores were smashed that thousands of Negro families could not get food for days after the riot.

neighborhoods most affected by the riot. The riot not withstanding, the ensuing years were an exciting time of new beginnings for black Detroiters. There were many firsts. Ralph Bunche, who lived his early years on the Near Eastside of Detroit, was awarded the Nobel Peace Prize in 1950 for his work mediating a peace plan between the Palestinians and the Israelis. Charles Thomas became the first black American to receive the Distinguished Service Cross for his heroism on December 1944. Rosa Slade-Gragg opened and operated the Slade-Gragg Academy of Practical Arts on a block that had been barred to commercial efforts in the past. Charles C. Diggs, Jr. became the first black from Michigan to be elected to the United States House of Representatives. The Detroit Lions hired their first black players. Ozzie Virgil became the first black to play for the Detroit Tigers. In 1955, Remus Robinson was the first black elected to serve on the Detroit Board of Education.

William Patrick, Jr.

The end of the war sparked a golden era for Detroiters. Industry flourished, but the focus was on consumer goods, i.e. cars, boats, refrigerators, all the things that made life easier and more pleasurable. The G I Bill gave many black veterans a chance to further their education and to purchase homes. Housing became more plentiful as whites sold their homes to the newly affluent blacks and began their move to the suburbs. Racial tensions appeared to be subsiding.

As their percentage of Detroit's population increased, blacks began to flex their economic and political muscle. With the personal support of UAW president, Walter P. Reuther and the efforts of the Trade Union Leadership Council TULC), in 1957 William Patrick became the first black elected to the Detroit City Council. The TULC, a powerful thirteen thousand-member group led by union activist, Horace Sheffield became the new economic and political power broker. These were good years to be alive and black in Detroit.

Horace Shefflield

This chapter has provided a brief overview of life on Detroit's Near Eastside, 1920-1960. The remaining chapters will take you on a journey back in time to the people and places of this era that, upon reflection, seems golden. The trip will be a fabulous one, enlightening and entertaining. Join us on this journey. Enjoy!

CHAPTER TWO
THE NEAR EASTSIDE NEIGHBORHOOD
OUR OWN SMALL PART OF THE UNIVERSE

There is an old West African proverb that says, "It takes a village to raise a child." The Near Eastside of Detroit **was** our "village." Within our village or community were many neighborhoods, linked by common bonds of race and religion. The neighborhoods were linked also by the universal desire and determination of the parents that their children would live in a larger world than they had known. Our parent's goal was not simply that their children would succeed in attaining a more fulfilled and productive life.

Our parents knew that there was a wider world than could be found in this 'village.' They inspired us to learn about the larger society, the world that had evaded them, and then encouraged us to go out and find or make our place in it. They knew that the achievement of a good education put one on the surest pathway to success in this society. Our families were our strongest support against the injustices of inequality and racism that were present in the larger society.

Community, like charity begins at home. This was never truer than on the Near East Side of Detroit. We know that children thrive only when their families thrive. In the 30's and beyond, many Near East Side residents were poor. In fact, much of the country suffered some degree of poverty. With everyone more or less in the same boat, people tended to help each other. It has been said that there is nobody more generous to the poor or needy than another poor person. This generosity was often tested.

Some families had relatives, aunts, uncles, and cousins, often living in the same house until they got "on their feet." Sometimes a family member came up from the South and joined their more 'affluent' family. At times these relatives may have been thought more of a liability than an asset. Yet who can deny that life can be more enjoyable, more emotionally satisfying, and a lot safer when one is part of a network of family, of friends and of a neighborhood?

Our community was more than an extension of our families. It was our bridge to the outside world. It was where we lived, worked and played. Neighbors knew that they needed each other in order to give their families the strength and determination to go out into the world and make a difference. Our friends' families became a part of our families. These relationships provided the safety net not always found in the larger society. As a result, deep and abiding friendships were formed, ones we will forever cherish.

There was no **one** neighborhood in the "village" we call the Near East Side. This "village" was made up of many neighborhoods. In this chapter, you will learn of some of the diverse neighborhoods within our "village" and of how these neighborhoods impacted on the lives of some of the residents.

Some will tell you, in their own words, what their life was like as they grew up on the Near East Side of Detroit. From their words, you will gain an understanding of why and of how so many achieved such excellence against the odds.

19

Alexanderine Street, Rivard Street and Forest Avenue

By
Joynal A. Muthleb

The Eastside neighborhood that our family lived on was a mixture of races and religions. The local drugstore and grocery store was owned and operated by a Jewish family. An Afro-American owned the dry cleaners. An Italian family owned the shoe repair shop. My father owned a restaurant that catered to families and factory workers. There were two restaurants operated by Asian families. The local grocery stores allowed residents to purchase their groceries on credit during the week. Usually on Friday {payday) the bill would be paid.

At this time, the entire area was a bustling scene of local commerce. We had all of the conveniences of a small city. In fact, people from the Far Eastside, the North End, Black Bottom and Conant Gardens would come to this area for some of their essential services. In addition to the commercial services, several doctor's offices, dentist's offices, and hospitals were located in his area.

Living on the Near Eastside was a unique experience. All of our needs as children and young adults were met within a one square mile area of our neighborhood. For recreation we had the Brewster Center, school playgrounds and the alleys as our play areas. For movies, we had the Garden Theater, the Forest Theater, the Willis Theater, and the Warfield Theater. Usually on Saturdays we would attend the Majestic Theater. At the Majestic Theater, admission was ten cents. The ten cents admission also entitled us to receive two comic books and a candy bar plus a double feature movie. Most of us paid our ten cents admission by returning empty pop bottles to the grocery store for the two cents bottle deposit.

The area was racially diverse. Italians, Jews, Slavs, and Afro-Americans lived as neighbors. The influx of Afro-Americans coming to Detroit to take advantage of work opportunities in the auto industry resulted in Afro-Americans becoming the majority population in the area. Generally, people who lived in our neighborhood were from "normal" families, but the area had its share of people that enjoyed the "sporting life."

All of us lived together in relative harmony.

Era J. Irving Williamson

20

Recollections of My Life on Medbury Street

By
Era J. Irving Williamson

I was one of seven children of Sam and Lela Irving. We lived at 587 Medbury Street over Mike's Grocery Store at the corner of St. Antoine and Medbury. We had a top front porch and in the summer; we would have overnight sleep over on the porch. Our street had a beautiful median or park that began at John R. Street and ran all the way to Russell Street. This was a very beautiful street of primarily large bricks homes, not always owned by the inhabitants. Buying a home was more difficult then because banks would not grant mortgages to black people.

In my family, it was mandatory for the children to visit the Detroit Art Museum and to use one's own library card to get books from the Main Public Library. In the summers, we went to 'Stay at Home Camp' at the YWCA. We would go every weekday and take our lunch. At the "Y' we would do Arts and Crafts and many kinds of sports and games and other activities. At the end of the day, we would go home and return happily the very next day.

My father worked at Ford Motor Company as a Master Plumber. My mother worked at Woolworth's Five and Dime store at Woodward and West Grand Boulevard as a dietitian. Some times my mother would work as a domestic.

When World War 11 broke out in 1941, my brother, Joc, was drafted in the Army. My father became an Air Raid Warden. After the war began, some foods were rationed, as were cigarettes and gasoline. Because of food shortages due to the feeding of the troops and the country's allies, food became more expensive. Some families had food bills at their local grocery where they could buy food and pay their bills when payday came around, usually on Friday.

Among my fondest memories, my father, called "Daddy" would get a big truck and fill it with hay and all of the kids would go for a Hay Ride at one of the parks. My mother loved picnics at Belle Isle. My father would take my brothers and go to the park at 4:00 a.m. in the morning and pick the right spot for our picnic and there we would be all day.

My parents would accompany my sister, Gloria, and my brother, Joe, to all of the dances at the Greystone Ballroom, where they would routinely win some of the Jitterbug contests. Our front porch was the hangout for the neighborhood kids and they would hang out on our steps. The reason for this was so that our parents would know where we were at all times.

The community in which I lived gave me a strong sense of family, of kinship. Neighbors took care of neighbors. I never knew or felt that I was poor because my parents raised my siblings and me as if we were what today are called "Middle Class."

———

Lela & Samuel Irving

Leland Street

By

Justine Rogers Wylie

In my young life, I grew up in a Detroit neighborhood where the streets were paved with cobblestone. This was Leland Street, a part of Old Detroit on the Near Eastside. On the corner of Leland and Rivard was a horse's trough. It was **not** for decoration. Horses and wagons were still fairly commonplace. Horses clip clopped down Leland with regularity, selling fruits and vegetables, delivering milk and orange juice, and selling "orange Ice," a most delicious sherbet, unlike any of the commercial sherbets sold today. Additionally, there were the "junk wagons," push or pull carts driven by manpower.

When your doorbell rang, there might be one of the bearded Orthodox Jewish men seeking *"old gold"* to buy. Alternatively, there might be one of the followers of "The Honorable Elijah Muhammad" seeking to popularize the brand of Islam espoused by him. One Muslim gentleman, a Mr. Curtis Pharr, was a regular if unwelcome visitor to our home. Mr. Pharr's stated aim was to convince my mother to wear long dresses and to cover her long and beautiful hair in the Muslim tradition, an idea that my mother considered ridiculous, but that my father perhaps secretly embraced. My father did not welcome Mr. Pharr because he believed that Pharr coveted my mother and would have liked her to become one of the several wives those "Black Muslims" were reported to have.

On winter days, we spent long hours by the radio listening to "The Hermit's Cave" or to "I Love a Mystery." We were still young enough to believe that *werewolves* existed. We believed whole heartily in Dracula and in ghosts. We believed in magic. My mother read all of the Grimm's fairy tales to us, so of course we believed in the existence of witches. In fact, I sometimes supposed that my mother, with her long, dark hair and her long nose might have been one. When we went to the Saturday movies at the Willis Theater on Willis and Hastings we saw Frankenstein, Dr. Jekyll and Mr. Hyde and

(L to R) Yvonne Rogers, Larry Rogers, Maruin Rogers & Justine Rogers.

the Zombies or the "Living Dead," so fascinating and so scary. Of course we also saw cowboys Tom Mix, Bob Steele, Roy Rogers and Gene Autry, but they lacked the power of the aforementioned.

Exciting goings on existed not far from our home. Sometimes there would be religious revivals in a big vacant lot across from the Willis Theater. These revivals took place under big tents, accompanied by much singing and shouting. I can remember being utterly mesmerized by a gorgeous woman, lying for an entire weekend in a glass coffin in a storefront window, supposedly alive but in a hypnotic trance. We visited her each day to see if she had awakened or if she was in fact, dead. I remember the "Tom Thumb Weddings" in which kindergarten aged children wore the formal dress of brides and grooms and had mock wedding celebrations at churches. Then there was Sunday school at New Bethel Baptist Church on Hastings Street at Willis that we Rogers kids attended. Being practical children, we would often take the money our parents gave us for the offering to buy Mary Janes, Squirrels, Tootsie Rolls and licorice sticks.

I recall vividly, the feelings of desolation on the day my father, recently laid off from his job, left Detroit and went to St. Louis where he had relatives who could help him find work to make enough money to provide for his family. I remember too, the absolute joy, the euphoria we felt when my father returned after a few short weeks and wrapped all four of his children inside of his big overcoat. I can remember him lifting my mother up in his arms as many kisses were exchanged. That was the last time my father ventured away from his family. Soon after his return, my father found a new job with better wages.

Certain diseases were prevalent during the thirties and forties, among them Diphtheria, Infantile Paralysis/ Polio and Scarlet Fever. All of them found their way into our neighborhood. Luckily, we escaped most of them due to the immunizations we received from our family physician and from the Public Health nurses who immunized children at school for Measles,

Lillie and Luther Rogers standing outside the Juvenile Detention Home, 1927.

Smallpox and Mumps. One day a Public Health nurse came to our house. After examining us kids, she posted a large yellow sign on our door that proclaimed in large letters, "QUARANTINE." This was a dreaded word in the 1930's. We knew it meant that no one could visit our house and that we could not attend school. It seemed that the two older siblings might have contracted Scarlet Fever although none of us displayed any apparent symptoms. Nor can I recall any specific medical treatment we received. After a few weeks, that same nurse revisited and examined us, removed the quarantine sign and our lives returned to normal.

I was young when our family moved from Leland Street and I did not carry my early friendships into my adulthood, yet I still remember the pride that black people felt because Joe Louis was the greatest prizefighter of his times, *and* he was *ours*. These were turbulent times, of large-scale unemployment and poverty and with the threat of war looming on the horizon. Yet these were the *growing years*, of kindergarten, of skate boxes, of Shirley Temple curls and of parents who loved each other *and* you. These were years full of promise of wonderful things to come.

————

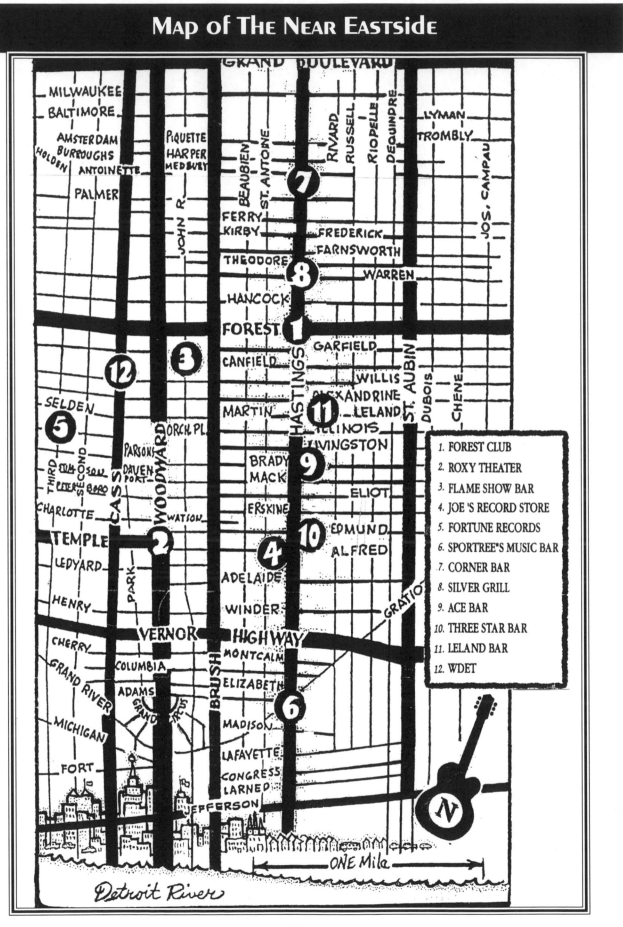

1. FOREST CLUB
2. ROXY THEATER
3. FLAME SHOW BAR
4. JOE'S RECORD STORE
5. FORTUNE RECORDS
6. SPORTREE'S MUSIC BAR
7. CORNER BAR
8. SILVER GRILL
9. ACE BAR
10. THREE STAR BAR
11. LELAND BAR
12. WDET

(Above) Looking NE on Erskine Street. (Below) The Children's Hospital 5224 St. Antoine.

Lenore Lewis Lawson, age 19. Taken by Ferguson Studio on Hasting Street.

The flourishing 'numbers' business played an important role in the neighborhood because 'playing the numbers' was one of the ways neighborhood people tried to beat the odds. Many pennies, nickels and dimes were gambled in hopes of making a killing on a number or numbers. We all knew the 'numbers' man and often shielded him from the police because we considered the numbers man a friend if not a neighbor.

Among Lenore's more glowing memories are:

■ Parading down Hastings Street banging pots and pans whenever Joe Louis won a boxing match

■ The backyard parties held by neighbors, that cost 25 cents to attend

■ Watching people looting stores along Hastings after or during the Race Riot of 1943.

Lenore Lawson's Mother

LENORE LEWIS LAWSON'S NEIGHBORHOOD

Lenore grew up on Hendrie Street with her parents, brothers and sisters just four houses from Hastings. Her recollections of those years that spanned the 1940's and 1950's are both vivid and tender.

Lenore in her memoirs writes, "I view my years growing up in the old neighborhood as some of the best years of my life. This was an area where we knew our neighbors and spoke to them by name. A time when we shared what we had with the other families from a cup of sugar to a dime for streetcar rides. Our neighborhood was special in the ways we looked out for each other and renting a spare bedroom was one of the way ends were met.

■   Dancing the Jitterbug at the Omega House on Ferry Street.

■   Spending Ration Stamps during World War II.

■   Saving paper, smashed cans and other items that were picked up for recycling for the 'War Effort.'

Mrs. Villars, a large, Caucasian woman teacher at Balch Elementary, respected and loved despite her stern demeanor because of her heart of gold

The music that filled her home, her school and her church that helped to make her world a joyful place.

Lenore writes, " I can truly say that our parents and friends thought we were poor but looking back in time, our love for family and friends were wealth beyond measure."

Justine Rogers Wylie

On Kirby Street

By
Justine Rogers Wylie

In 1941, our family moved to East Kirby. This was our best house. It had a large back porch and a larger front porch. In our big back yard were two apple trees, two pear trees and a Black Walnut tree. We would climb on the concrete garbage can, hoist ourselves upon the garage and lie on the roof of the garage to sun and plan and dream. The bravest of us would lie on the walnut tree's big branches and sunbathe. We could eat as many pears as we wanted, and use what pears that were left as bargaining tools to trade for other kids bounty. We would eat all the apples we could manage to eat, yet there were always enough apples for my mother to use for making applesauce, apple jelly and apple butter. We could make powerful and lasting stains on our hands and feet from the coating on the black walnuts. These stains were about all that we derived from the black walnut trees because the meat of the walnuts was never quite edible.

.   On the front, looking south was a large sloping lawn leading to the sidewalk. Beyond the sidewalk was a grassy median with two Dutch Elm trees that we loved. These trees were our landmarks. We played under them and around them. These trees were the starting point for our games. "Hide and Go Seek" began there as did "Follow the Leader" and "Pump, Pump Pied Away." Later we fought to save these same trees when Dutch elm disease invaded the area and began destroying the trees in the neighborhood. All of the Rogers kids grew to adulthood in this house. Two of them married from this house. We were happy there.

.

Two blocks east of our house was a Yugoslav / Serbian community from which many of the children came. I had never heard of Serbia, but I knew where Yugoslavia was located on the world map at school. I later learned that the Yugoslavian and Serbian people were basically the same people but that this didn't make them like each other. Many of these people were Muslim; others were Coptic Christians or Catholic.

These Slavic people occupied three corners of Kirby and Russell. On two of these corners were coffee houses or restaurants. Men in dark suits, smoking, drinking, eating and playing cards and board games populated them. It would have taken more courage than I had to enter such an establishment. I never heard them speak English. I wanted to know what they were saying. I wanted to know where they came from and what games they were playing. I wondered whether these men had wives. They were seldom seen with women. I fantasized about the large, round deep-dish pie pans filled with veggies, meats and cheeses sitting enticingly in the windows. These pies looked intriguing and perhaps delicious. We never knew! I was not alone in believing that these men used their native language to prevent outsiders from hearing the racist remarks they were perhaps making. That may have my paranoia. Today, I believe that they were perhaps just more comfortable speaking their native language.

The northwest corner of Kirby and Russell was the home of the Yugoslav Grocery Store owned by one of few men who demonstrated the ability to speak English. He was a large, somewhat swarthy complexioned man whose arms were covered with thick, dark hair. This was the grocery where we bought large dill pickles from a huge barrel on the sawdust-covered floor. This is also where we purchased our meats and vegetables. This was really a beautiful store, lovingly tended by the owner. Shopping in this market was a treat.

As children, much of our lives revolved around the immediate family followed by school friends and extended family and family friends. My father was a part of a large extended family, a family of many cousins who lived on Rivard between Ferry and Kirby. These cousins lived in conjoined housing with a large common area in the back, which we would flood in the cold winter months for ice-skating. The cousins all attended the same church, Scott Methodist Episcopal on East Kirby and St. Antoine, the church where family weddings and funerals were held. The elders believed in the adage," the family that prays together, stays together." Holidays were often celebrated together with backyard cookouts and family picnics. The family unity was derived largely from the fact that this close-knit family was of one branch. They had been born and raised initially in Oktibbeha County in rural Mississippi and had migrated to Michigan in the early 1920's.

I had three good friends, Marlene Grice, a diminutive copy of myself, except that she owned a

Typical Two-family Flat on Kirby Street.

full size girls bicycle and I didn't. Then there was Elizabeth Lazroi, a Serbian, and Violet Kristich, a Yugoslavian. Violet was tall and blond and very pretty. Her family owned a superb bakery at Riopelle and Kirby. For many years, my family bought breads hot from the oven from this bakery. Elizabeth Lazroi was small, dark and quietly fun. These three girls were my best friends at Garfield Elementary School. As we entered puberty, our relationships changed. Elizabeth Lazroi's family moved from the neighborhood to Dearborn where many Muslim families lived. Violet Kristich transferred to an Orthodox Catholic school in the neighborhood. Her family's bakery remained for many years.

There were other friends and neighbors that enriched our young lives. Among them was the Boyce family of five boys and two girls. The three younger boys, Robert, Charles and James were a rambunctious group, tall in stature, spirited and very loquacious. They were *The Three Musketeers* of Kirby Street. They were admired for their chutzpah, their cohesiveness and their athletic abilities.

On a Sunday in July 1943, there was news on the radio of a "Race Riot." . The rumor was spread that a white man had thrown a black child off of the Belle Isle Bridge. Alternatively, it was reported that a black woman had been raped by a group of white men. This was strong stuff and very scary. Stores were being broken into and looted. Sporadic gunfire could be heard in the distance. There was much automobile traffic and what I remember as truckloads of people driving through the neighborhood shouting racial epithets and threats aimed at both races. For the next few days, we were afraid to venture from our home. It was alleged to be dangerous and foolhardy to cross Woodward Avenue.

After a few days, we Rogers kids decided that it was time to venture out into the neighborhood. The first building that we visited was McFall's Funeral Home on the southwest corner of Canfield and Hastings. I'm not sure if one can stroll and be surreptitious at the same time, but pre riot, we kids would visit the funeral home as if we had business there. We would look at the guest register, proceed to the viewing room and stare at the one or two bodies that always seemed to be on view. Macabre little creatures that we were, we would study the bodies, speculate on the ages of the deceased and note the relative plainness or opulence of the caskets. On this post riot day, when we arrived at McFalls, we were absolutely astounded and dismayed at what we saw. Instead of the usual one or two bodies, there were seven! Men and women in caskets had filled the viewing room and spilled out into the anteroom. Reportedly, these deaths were riot related. After that day, we seldom visited the funeral home. The dead had lost their charm

The riot of 1943 sparked the beginning of changes that affected the demographics of the neighborhood. This was perhaps the beginning of "White Flight." Following the riot, businesses were rebuilt and flourished on the near eastside of Detroit. The changes in the demographics seemed to make little difference in the lives of the neighbors. Children grew up, married and moved from the neighborhood. Families relocated to northern areas of the city. Years later, it took the *monster* Chrysler Freeway a very few short years to destroy what had taken the area many decades to build.

––––––––

Marvin Wayne Rogers

29

| Dorothy Greenfield Hill | John Harris Hill, Sr. |

Warren Avenue and the Surrounding Neighborhood

By
Dorothy Greenfield Hill

I was born at 5020 St. Antoine and Warren on the site that is now Plymouth United Church of Christ. My father was owner of the Eagle Moving Company, a home-based business that was housed the basement of our building. Our family lived on the first floor and rented out the second floor. Our home was part of a terrace building that reached to Warren and Hastings.

Though I lived on the Cross-town Streetcar and the Oakland Streetcar lines, I was a great walker. Because my home was centrally located, I would walk to school, both to the Trowbridge Elementary, the Garfield Intermediate, Northeastern High School and Wayne State University.

Walking was not only a pleasure, but instructive. It gave me the opportunity to see and to know intimately, much of the neighborhood. There was C.T. Collins' flower shop as I walked west on Warren. There were churches, Bethel A.M.E. on Frederick and St. Antoine and Plymouth Congregational on Garfield and Beaubien. The Warfield Theater was only a hop, skip and a jump away from my home. The Gordy family grocery store on St. Antoine and Frederick was one of several neighborhood grocery stores.

Unlike today, most people felt safe walking in the community alone. Hastings Street was thriving with grocery stores, shoe repair shops and a Barthwell's Ice Cream Parlor where ice cream was plentiful, delicious and cost only a nickel. This was a time when people would be sitting on stoops and felt free to talk to perfect strangers. Neighbors kept a watchful eye on each other's property, especially their children.

I remember when Joe Louis knocked out Max Schmelling to win the World Heavyweight Boxing Championship. Neighbors came out cheering, car horns blowing. The whole community celebrated. Black people had a champion! Joe Louis' accomplishments as a boxer gave a sense of pride to the community. I remember too, the "Race Riot" of 1943 when Hastings Street was a fearful place to be because of the pillaging and burning of businesses and the massive police presence.

Despite the hustle and bustle of the business and entertainment community, there was a strong feeling of unity within the community. We respected each other and there was a feeling of security and peace.

Medbury Avenue

By
Teola P. Hunter

Teola Cranon Hunter

I was born into a warm and wonderful family yes, but I was also born into a neighborhood. My neighborhood was endowed with beautiful people, poor but proud, determined to live their lives as fully as possible. Living on Medbury Avenue, I was privy to a host of wonderful things. There was the Art Museum just a few blocks away where one could visit and muse and learn about other histories and cultures. One could view mummies from ancient Egypt and a skeleton lying in a glass coffin. One could go to the Main Public Library and attend story hour where a storyteller told or read tales of wonderment and of enchantment. I attended a marvelous school, the Balch Elementary. A magnificent school with its tremendous playground and the only swimming pool in a Detroit Public elementary school

What was called " family" was sometimes not family at all. Almost everyone close was claimed as a cousin. We had "play sisters" and "play brothers." We knew everyone in the block and beyond. It seemed that most parents had a stake

in other's children, looking out for their welfare and trying to keep them from the "devilment" that children do. It was not unusual for children who stayed overnight to sleep on a pallet on the floor. Many families had a kind of credit account at the neighborhood stores where they could get groceries when they ran out of money between paydays. Many parents played the numbers in hope of hitting it big. Some few did. You didn't have to leave the neighborhood to find good friends. You didn't have to leave the neighborhood to find many things that most people wanted or needed. It is a blessing to be able to say that some of the friends of my childhood have turned out to be friends for life.

My father, T.P. Crannon, was a young man when he developed kidney problems, but he was born too soon to benefit from the modern day technology of dialysis. He died on December 23rd, 1938 at the age of 40. Our family had not experienced the wrath of the depression when my father was alive and working for Ford Motor

Teola Cranon

I can't remember going to bed in a cold house, but I do remember the coal stove in the dining room.

I don't ever remember not having a bed to sleep in, but I can remember sharing a bed with my sister. Now, I often wonder where my mother slept.

I can't remember not having clothes to wear, but I do remember my older siblings being the recipients of used clothes from families my mother worked for.

I don't ever remember not having new patent leather shoes for winter or T straps for Mother's Day, but I do remember my mother wearing the same oxfords year in and year out.

Years later, my mother upgraded her skills and became a custodial worker for the Detroit Public Schools. Because of her observations of and admiration for the teachers she encountered in the classrooms, she persuaded me to become a teacher.

My mother died in 1971 before I had received my Master's Degree.

———

Company. Without his salary, our family was officially poor for the first time, but survive we did under the stewardship of our strong mother.

My mother worked outside of the home to augment our meager income. She wanted her children to live an abundant life. I observed my mother throughout the years working; struggling and suffering to assure that her children would have the best that she could provide. Because my mother had little formal education or training, she knew firsthand the results of a lack of a good education, and she encouraged, emphasized, even pounded into our heads daily, the value of education.

I don't remember not having food to eat, but I can remember accompanying my mother as she pulled a little wagon to get food subsidies.

I don't recall a Christmas without some special gift I wanted, but I do remember getting boxes from the Goodfellows.

Marjorie Shephard

My Life on Medbury Street

By
Marjorie Shephard Davidson

Until 1953 when the I-94 Freeway (Edsel Ford) was being built, my parents, Millidge and Minnie Kate Shephard, my brother Millidge Jr. and I lived in a terrace apartment at 514 Medbury on the southeast corner of Medbury and Beaubien. The terrace was a three-story building with two apartments on the first and second floor, and one apartment on the third floor. On each floor was a common bathroom. The first floor bathroom had a stall shower and the second floor bathroom had a bathtub. No kids ever lived on the third floor so I never saw that bathroom. Each family kept their toilet paper, soap, towels and Roman Cleanser for clean up in their own apartments. Our apartment had one bedroom where my parents slept. My brother and I shared a "Roll-Away" bed until I was eleven years old. At age eleven, I was given the bed all to myself. My brother then slept in the living room on a duo-fold couch.

My father worked at Capital Poultry Market located at 1416 East Vernor Highway in the Eastern Market district. He worked there all of my life until he became disabled in 1961. He was known around the market as "Shep" or "Slim." All of the poultry was alive in wooden pens located in the store and also in the front of the store on the street. The storeowners, Miss Rosie and Mr. V. were very good to our entire family. Mr. V. saw to it that my father always had a used car. He also sold him an outboard boat, which looked like the rental canoes on Belle Isle.

A park divided Medbury Street with sidewalks on each side running from St. Antoine to Beaubien. On the corner of Medbury and Beaubien was a water fountain. My mother told me not to drink from the fountain because the "Junk Men" let their horses drink from it. There was a green wooden building in the park where the adults voted called "The Voting Booth." My buddies and I would write on the building with our hopscotch chalk. We would skate in the park on our ball bearing roller skates, skate keys hanging around our necks. I wanted to skate at The Forest Club where the kids were black and the music was lively, but Hastings Street was off limits to me. We also rode our Schwinn bicycles; made mud pies, played Hide & Seek, Kick the Can and Jacks.

During the war, we bought war stamps. When the stamp book was filled up, the owner(s) received a $25.00 war bond, and a soldier would come to the school in a jeep and ride the kids around the playground as a reward for buying the bond. When the war ended, people riding on the Oakland street car hung out of the streetcar windows, waving flags in celebration of the war's ending.

―――――――

George Ramsey (right & inset), Ron Milner Center on Warren Avenue.

MY STREET of DREAMS

By
George D. Ramsey, Sr.

I was born at 952 E. Warren Avenue between Hastings and Rivard on April 8, 1938 where I lived the first 18 years of my life. Hastings Street was the corridor that black businesses thrived on. Warren Avenue too, had its share of Black Enterprise.

Victory Mutual Insurance was at 253 E. Warren, The Tom Phillips Post was at 269 E. Warren and Cole's Funeral Home was at 275 E. Warren. My buddies and I would venture over to Cole's and peep through the basement windows to see the bodies laid out to be dressed or to be embalmed. This block between Brush and John R. was also where Ziggy Johnson's Dance Studio and the office of Joe Louis's physician {Dr. Bob Bennett) was located. The Charles Wright Museum of African American History now stands on this block. .

The four storied "Booker T. apartment at 429-431 E. Warren between Brush and Beaubien was where some of my schoolmates lived. Some of the more daring fellows would jump across their rooftops to the adjacent buildings. That is, until one fellow didn't quite make the jump, but by the grace of God was able to grab the gutters and break his fall. He broke his leg, but survived the fall!

Across the street at 446 E. Warren was the Detroit Memorial Building with its many black businesses. It housed the East Side Medical Lab, the Booker T. Washington Trade Association, the NAACP, the Visiting Nurses Association and the Detroit Memorial Park Corporation where my mother purchased funeral plots for my brother, Archie Jr., my father, Archie Sr., as well as her father, John Oliver. On 458 E. Warren was the White Star Grill, the first sit down restaurant that I remember my mother taking me to. A friend of my mother worked there and she treated my mother and me to a meal. that my mother's finances could not afford.

Between St. Antoine and Hastings was Dean Nolan's School of Music at 552 E. Warren and I remember him asking my mother to allow me to take lessons from him. I had no interest in doing so because of the rumors about his sexual preferences. The Michigan Federated Democratic Club at 613 E. Warren was where my singing group sang for Charles C. Diggs Jr. when he ran for the United States Congress. This was the first time I was able to get past the front door without being chased out. One of Detroit's most respected "numbers men" lived on "My Street of Dreams."

But, my fondest memories are of the 900 block, my block, where death and despair was always near and where musical dreams were "nourished and where they flourished." Such as the very first day the Cross town Trolley ran down Warren Avenue and we witnessed its first victim. Earlier that day, a drunken man had stepped in front of the trolley and was run over on the corner of Hastings in front of the Warren Avenue 5 & 10 cent store at 903 E. Warren. I came out of the five and dime and when I crossed Warren Avenue; I had to step over parts of his brain that still lay near the curb. Agnes Thornton White, a childhood friend who lived at 937 E. Warren, often talked with me about the incident because she and her mother had to step over his remains on their way to the bus stop. Next door, the Astoria Bar and Tavern at 915 E. Warren was where the police shot a man they had chased into the hotel side of the building. He came back out bleeding from his wounds and sat down on a brick pedestal that was in front of the hotel. When they took him away, his blood lay on the street as a remainder of him until the rains came and washed the blood from "My Street of Dreams."

In the flat above my family at 954 E. Warren lived Andrew Harkless, a trumpeter (Spirit of Swing), a big band started at Miller High School in 1939. Andrew often practiced his playing in our shared basement or on his back porch. I spent many days with his mother, sitting at the kitchen table with a glass of milk eating homemade cookies as she drank Sanka coffee and listening to his muted playing before he left to serve in the US Navy during WW11. He was my first inspiration to want to play an instrument, which I did, but never as well as my to be remembered neighbor.

Will Davis, a noted jazz [pianist, played and recorded with Sonny Stitt's group) Lord Nelson and his Boppers) in 1948. He also played with the group that included Milt Jackson, Yusef Laateef and with Charlie (Yardbird) Parker when he played at the Crystal Bar on Grand River and Lawton. It gave us bragging rights, Will with Bird in a black and tan! Will lived at 990 E. Warren with his mother and sister, Audrey. He was as cool as the music he played. I spent many evenings on his mother's porch eating peaches from their bountiful peach tree as he filled the air with melodies while his sister combed my hair. I was one of his mother's favorite kids on "My Street of Dreams."

Floyd Taylor, one of Detroit's "boogie woogie" pianists lived across the street at 987 E. Warren. Floyd worked for the city as a garbage man. He, his wife Velma and daughter Beverly shared their home with Velma's' mother, Hattie Campbell, a loving person and probably one of my mother's closest friends. Her husband and my father had been "drinking buddies." They treated me like I was family. Mrs. Campbell dipped snuff and I begged her to let me try it. She did and when I swallowed some of the juice and gagged, she laughed and I swore never to dip snuff, and I never did. She told my mother and they laughed a lot over it.

Floyd was a legendary player in the "spots" where he played with many of the top musicians. Yusef Lateef was a sideman in one of his bands during the early 50's. Floyd played in Paul Williams band and on his recordings, All the Boys for the Ride" and "Paradise Valley Walk." In 1948, Williams recorded his biggest hit, "The Hucklebuck." I remember Floyd opening the door as he played with the record while my friends and I danced on the porch in absolute delight. Jerry Jennings and his wife Odesse who lived with the Livingstons in the upper flat (985) delighted the crow by "Doing the Hucklebuck' in their front yard. It was indeed a block party on "My Street of Dreams."

My friend Wilbert Anderson lived at 1003 E. Warren with his aunt whose husband, Mr. Green, sang with the "Detroiters," a gospel group. We knew they traveled singing and their songs were played in record shops along Hastings on Sunday mornings. He was a real celebrity! When he walked down the street, he received the adulation that he deserved. He was sharp and his group was great looking and soundings. This was the group that first caught my attention and impressed me. They were really the group, which made me want to be a Do Wopper, which I did become. I was surrounded by the dynamics and the atmosphere that bred musical greatness in an era that showed great things were and could be realized on Warren Avenue, "My Street of Dreams."

———

Some Recollections of Almeta Carruth Reid White

I lived in the Fernando Apartment Building at 607 E. Adams on the corner of Adams and St. Antoine from 1950-1957 from the age of 15 to 22 with my parents, Fred and Almeta Carruth, caretakers for this 14 unit building owned by the Fred G. Nagel Company and also for the Diamond Drugstore located at Gratiot and Hastings.

Some of the tenants in this building were: Chester Rentee, also known as "Mayor of Paradise Valley" on the 2nd floor, Azelia Ewing who lived behind her beauty shop on the 1st floor, Maceo Campbell who had a Cleaning and Pressing Shop in the basement, Dr. Lee (Tip Lee) who lived behind his office in a basement apartment, Attorney Chester Rhodes and his wife, Maybelle, who lived on the 1st floor in the apartment behind his office. Mrs. Rhodes wrote social columns for the Pittsburgh Courier.

Almeta Carruth White

Some things I remember are:
Saturday walks to the Eastern Market to shop, going to Canada to buy meat, watching the Thanksgiving Parade floats come up St. Antoine and turn west on Adams going back to the J.L. Hudson's Warehouse, walking downtown to shop, hanging out on the playground in back of the Lucy Thurman Y, our family's 1st TV and "The Big Four Police."

Some places I remember:
On Adams Street going toward Hastings was the Palmer House, the Abalon Hotel, the Horseshoe Lounge with a wonderful organ player, the 602, a gambling place above the cleaners on the corner, Paradise Bowl, an ice cream parlor on Hastings at the end of Adams called Fan Tan's, Goldberg's Drugstore on the corner of Adams and St. Antoine, and Stroh's Brewery Truck place.

My church was and still is Sacred Heart on Eliot and Rivard, so I walked Hastings a lot going to and from activities. I passed places like Barthwell's Drug Store, Dr. E. Chester Hedgemans's office, Castle Theater and Diggs

Funeral Home. When we got to Forest & Hastings, I remember one of the Oakland Bus Drivers would call out," Old Age Pension, Juvenile Detention, Welfare and ADC to the right. Of course, I didn't know this was a ghetto.

These seven years were some of the best years of my life. This is not boasting, just giving credit to how a village can raise a child. In 1952, I managed to graduate from one of the top Catholic Girls Schools; Immaculata High, which is now Bates Academy. This was the second class to have black graduates. In 1960, I graduated from Mercy College with a B.S. in what is now called, Health Information Management.

In 1957, I married Carter Marshall Reid who lived in the Brewster Projects and who attended grade school with me at Sacred Heart. We had two children together.

———

The Lamar Family

(As Told To Justine Wylie)

There is said to be an old African belief that so long as a person is remembered, they still live. Only when they are forgotten and their names are no longer spoken are they finally gone.

I am Anne Elizabeth Lamar Daniels, a member of a family that seems destined for extinction. I am writing this to ensure that my family's life history be evidences that they, we did indeed live and that someone, somewhere will remember us and speak our names.

I was born and lived on the northwest corner of St. Antoine St. and Willis on Detroit's Near Eastside. We lived upstairs in the back of a storefront apartment building. I was one of four boys and two girls born to Nelson and Helen Taylor Lamar. Born also into this family were twin boys, Lamar Lamar and Lapar Lamar. A midwife, Aloma Robinson, delivered them but neither survived infancy. We were all born in the era of The Great Depression. We were poor as was almost everyone we knew.

My father was born in Georgia, my mother in Alabama. My father was an old man when they married. The only paid employment that I remember him having was a job with the WPA. My father was a poor man, not an attractive man, and was known to use alcohol to excess on occasion. Yet, my mother was his in body if not in spirit. When we were older, we wondered how this old man, our father, could have won the heart of our vivacious and talented mother. Perhaps it was because of his elegant and eloquent speaking style. He was beautifully articulate and knew the bible better than he knew his children. All of us went to New Bethel Baptist Church, where my father, always addressed as Mr. Lamar, was often called upon to deliver a eulogy or speak for the family of a deceased. We were quite proud of him on those occasions.

My mother was gifted with an indomitable spirit and many talents. She was very beautiful to us. She could take the worst looking head of hair and turn it into a thing of beauty with just a straightening iron and hot curlers. She was a marvelous cook. Cakes, pies, salmon croquettes and many pots of peas and beans were often in our kitchen. And she could dance, oh how she could dance! We had an old fashioned RCA Victrola, unique in this neighborhood. My mother could do the Big Apple, the Lindy Hop, the Jitterbug and any other dance that emerged. We would mimic her, dancing around the room following her steps and getting in her way. I remember that Lil Green and Jay McShan's orchestra were her favorite musicians. All the neighbors' children loved to come to our house.

For reasons only the creator knows, ours was a family bound for extinction. First my second oldest brother Leon, died, then my father, next my oldest brother, Walter, and finally, the younger three, Nelson, Raymond and Nella. I am the only survivor and barely, the victim of a massive heart attack. To my knowledge and against all odds, only one of the six children who lived to adulthood had progeny and his sexual preferences would seem to preclude offspring. It is my hope that someone, somewhere will remember us and speak our name and that we will not be forgotten.

Nelson, Jr   Anne   Walter

Nelson Lamar, Sr. And Nella   Helen

Raymond   Leon

37

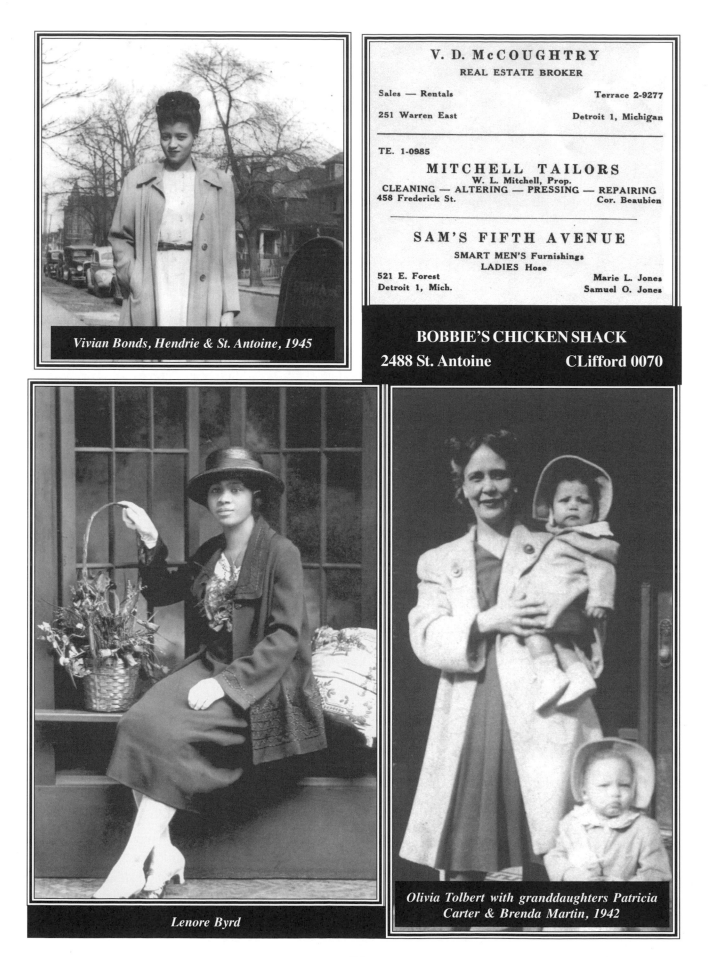

Vivian Bonds, Hendrie & St. Antoine, 1945

Lenore Byrd

*Olivia Tolbert with granddaughters Patricia
Carter & Brenda Martin, 1942*

The Warfield Theater, Hastings Street at Farnsworth, 1936

Evelyn Delaney's 16th Birthday Party

Guests and Honoree include Evelyn Delaney, Mrs. Annie Delaney, Gwendolyn Delaney, Rae Annette Lightsey, Devera Lightsey, Willie Mae Brown, Marilyn McComb, Nancy McComb, Gloria Irving, Calvin White, Marcus Burden, Eloise Porter, Lois Irving, Aunt Lizzy, and Teola Cranon.

40

Friends following a football game between Northeastern and Northwestern High Schools.
Standing L to R, Unk, Unk, Marlene Grice, Yvonne rogers, Luther Rogers, Sally Bean
Lower Front, L to R, June Bonner, Frances Grice.

41

Eugene U. Elzy, Jr.

Sylvia Braithwaite & Portia Conway, Joe Louis Farm, Utica, MI, 1948.

The Henry Family on Belle Isle. Eula (2nd from left), her husband Willie (C) and their three sons (L to R) John, Robert and Charles.

Wilbur Lenox, Terry Bagwell & Nathan McAlpin
Neighborhood Picnic, 1953.

Theodore Phillips & Jean Everage
Medbury Park.

Ruth Irma Jackson & Rose Young
On Beaubien St., 1942.

Aaron Fox, Nelson Fox & Jimmy Collins
Beaubien St., 1940.

Willa Bee Cox

Inell Martin

Shirley Lewis, Coranell Rowlette & Florence Rowlette (1945).

Mrs. Redding (L) & Her Son, Clarence (R), Medbury Street, (1940's).

Mrs. Julia Everage Enjoying Belle Isle.

Anita Cosley

45

Ruth E. Jackson & Shirley Lewis

Gloria Irving In Front of Larks Drug Store.

Leroy Stewart & Coranell Roulette

Ruth Irma, Alonzo Edgar & Yvonne Smith

Chapter Three
The Near Eastside Schools

There was a time when "Black is beautiful" was an unknown concept; a time when it appears that no serious thought was given to the significance of portraying black families in the elementary text books in the hope that beginning readers would identify with the characters and perhaps be inspired to learn and read about people who looked like themselves. There was a time when little thought seemed to be given to the importance of African-American teachers as role models. The role models that many of the children born in the decades of the 20's through 40's knew best were sports figures, like Joe Louis and Jesse Owens or musicians such as Cab Calloway and Duke Ellington. It is probable that some of us were told of George Washington Carver and his experiments with the peanut. Some few of us will have heard of the big debate between W.E. B. Dubois and Booker T. Washington over the relative value of vocational education as opposed a more traditional academic curriculum or the so called "talented tenth" theory of education for blacks in American society.

Whether one was the victim or the beneficiary of the progressive educational system that existed then, there is one abiding truth. Black parents knew the value of education. They knew that education was the surest way to achieve economic success and its entitlements. Under-educated themselves, they were determined that their children receive at least a high school education. The phrase that arose in the Black Power Movement, "by any means necessary" very aptly and accurately describes what parents were willing to do to ensure that their sons and daughters received the education that so many of them had been denied. They were convinced that education was the solution, that it would open the door to a more fulfilled life and to the achievement of the American dream.

The public elementary schools on the Near East Side included the Lincoln School, the Bishop School, the Trowbridge School, the Russell School and the Balch School. Garfield School was both an elementary and junior high or intermediate school. There was also two Catholic schools, Sacred Heart and Holy Rosary. No public high school existed within our defined borders, but Northeastern was the school of choice for many of the Near East Side high school kids. Others attended Northern, Northwestern or Cass Technical High School. Although Miller High School was in closer proximity to and was well known to the Near East Side residents, it was avoided for the most part because it was primarily a black school located in a neighborhood that was considered less safe.

When Near East Side students attended athletic events that included Miller High School, it seemed that Miller students exhibited more spirit and perhaps more joy in their competitiveness. The cheerleaders were sassier and shapelier than those from Northeastern. Their lyrics were more daring, their moves more rhythmic. What appeared to be an extra hustle in the athletes excited the students. Some of us envied the cohesiveness that comes from being part of a school that was relatively homogenous, both racially and economically.

Yet, whether bold or shy, we took to our more integrated schools with a vengeance, our parents' dreams for us becoming our dreams. No stranger to racism and to segregationist practices in Detroit, we took the extra steps needed and we accomplished what had eluded so many of our parents. We received our high school diplomas!

The Lincoln Elementary School

The original Lincoln School was built in 1872 and was named in honor of our 16th President, Abraham Lincoln. The Lincoln School that some of us attended opened in 1913 with an annex added in 1917. It has been said that if any person is new to the city and has his goal, the location of the 'Black Community,' that person should simply ask for the location of the Lincoln School and he will find what he is seeking. This may not always have been so, but the Detroit Public School archives tell us that in 1872, black citizens of Detroit petitioned the Board of Education to name Mrs. Sarah A. Cook as a teacher of their people. Mrs. Cook had been employed from February 1870 to June, 1872 as a provisional teacher in the Ohio Street School that was the predecessor of the original Lincoln School. The school board denied the petition to give a more permanent status to Mrs. Cook, ostensibly on the basis that Mrs. Cook did not have the required certification to be more than a provisional teacher. The board also negated the assumption that the Ohio Street School had been or that the new Lincoln School was to be a distinctive "colored school".

We have no knowledge of how many prominent Detroiters attended Lincoln Elementary School in Detroit. What we do know is that the demographics of African-Americans on the Near East Side in earlier Detroit insures that a numerically significant number of those who later achieved prominence attended the Lincoln School at some time.

The Trowbridge Elementary School

In 1883, on Forest Avenue between St. Antoine and Hastings, an elementary school was built in honor of General Luther S. Trowbridge, Civil War Hero, practicing attorney and distinguished public servant of the City of Detroit and the State of Michigan. In 1889 the site was

Trowbridge Elementary School

48

enlarged to become what we knew as the Trowbridge School. It was a two-story brick building that had a seating capacity for five hundred seventy students. The racial composition of the original school is not known, but by 1937, 94.7% of the student population was black or African-American.

Mrs. Dorothy V. Hill, a retired teacher from the Detroit Public Schools, says of the Trowbridge School, "My career dream was born at Trowbridge. I would become a teacher and try to touch and inspire my students to become the best they could become, like the teachers at Trowbridge inspired me." Mrs. Hill speaks also of her first visit back to Trowbridge as a substitute teacher after her graduation from Wayne State University. She says, "It was such an eerie feeling. I went back in time and saw myself as a five year old. I sensed the excitement the children felt. I hoped that kindergarten would be for them what it had been for me, a joyful experience and the beginning of a lifetime of learning."

Joynal Muthleb speaks, not only of fond memories of his years at Trowbridge, but also of the profoundly positive influence his experiences as a student have had on his adult life. Joynal attributes his life-long love and appreciation of classical music to the hours he spent listening to classical music written by the masters and played on 78 rpm records in the classroom of music teacher, Ms. Thelma Williams. He credits Mrs. Beulah Brewer, his auditorium teacher, for encouraging and nurturing his interest in stage productions and his participation in group activities. Of William Loving, gym teacher, Joynal says, " Mr. Loving had a talent for building self-confidence in his students. I vividly remember his insistence that students wear dress shirts in school. He would always say, 'Wear a tie with your shirt. And if you don't have a tie, put a shoestring around your neck.' Wearing a tie to school became part of my dress code through high school and beyond."

———

Balch Elementary School, 5536 St. Antoine.

The Balch Elementary School

When the Balch School was opened in 1921 on the east side of St. Antoine between Ferry and Palmer, a star was born. It was the only elementary school with a swimming pool. Swimming instruction was mandatory for all students starting with the 4th grade. It was the first building designed especially for the platoon system that had become newly popular. Balch was also the first elementary school with rooms designed for use by the community. The uniqueness of Balch elementary attracted educators from all over this country and from abroad. It was adjacent to the Goldberg Athletic Field, an area so large that minor league baseball players would practice on what was commonly thought of as the Balch playground.

Balch school was named for George Washington Balch, a Michigan transplant from New York State who had a distinguished career in private enterprise and also in public office. Mr. Balch was president of the Detroit Common Council, a member of the Detroit Board of Education and a member of the Board of Health. Additionally, he was one of the incorporators of the Detroit Museum of Art.

The original student enrollment was approximately 96% Jewish. When the Jewish families moved to the northwestern areas of Detroit, black families moved into the neighborhood. By 1936, 96% of the student body was black. In an attempt to meet the needs of the changing population, an Open Air room was established in 1928. By 1932, a Special "A" room was opened. Open Air rooms were established to serve the frail children who were underweight, underfed, or were suffering from a chronic condition that made participation in a regular school program not easily possible. In the Open Air rooms, dietitians provided nutritionally correct breakfasts and lunches. Nurses and social workers were a part of the Open Air staff. This was a time when Tuberculosis and Polio, then called Infantile Paralysis was not at all uncommon. Special A was designed to serve the needs of the mildly retarded or special needs children who were educable, but could not thrive in a regular classroom. In practice, Special A was sometimes used as a dumping ground for children who were difficult to manage in the classroom and/or who prevented other children from achieving their maximal potential because of disruptive behavior.

One of the Near Eastsiders, Era Williamson, describes Balch as "an outstanding elementary school. She remembers Mrs. Villars, a music teacher, as one of the best teachers at Balch. Williamson says of Mrs. Villars, "We were introduced to the Masonic Temple by her. Because of her teachings, we learned all of the instruments that were played in a classical symphony orchestra."

Another Near Eastsider recalls Balch School and its playground as providing some of her fondest and most vivid memories. Included among these memories are the summer recreation programs and the softball games that all of the neighborhood folks went to. Ernie Wagner, former Globetrotter, credits the recreation instructor at the Balch School playground as the catalyst for his interest in and the development of his athletic skills.

The Garfield Elementary School

The Garfield School, named after James Abram Garfield, president of Hiram College, major general in the Civil War, member of the U.S. Congress and Senate from Ohio, and later, Republican President of the United States, was opened in 1888 on Rivard Street and Frederick Avenue. A frame structure, it was replaced by a larger brick building in 1898. As the school population grew, additional property was purchased that extended the school site to Kirby Avenue. In 1915, an annex was built that contained sixteen rooms. By 1923, when an addition to the building was completed, the original staff of eight teachers had grown to seventy. Corridors connected the original building, the annex and the new addition. What began as a kindergarten through fifth grade school, with the opening of the new addition, became a kindergarten through eighth grade school.

One former student says of the Garfield Elementary School, "What a school it was! For

Garfield Elementary School

me, it was the school from heaven! It lacked nothing but a swimming pool and an ice skating rink. There were two playgrounds and two gymnasiums. There were weird and wonderful teachers. There were great cooks in the cafeteria kitchen that would bake wonderful yeast breads and rolls for lunch. There was an engineer who kept a large cat as a companion. There was a horde of kids, different, funny and fun." The 'different' kids were the ones who came from the Yugoslav/Serbian enclave just east of Garfield. These first generation Americans lacked the rambunctious energy of the black children, yet they were quietly fun and seemed to have a calming effect on the more spirited students.

Though only a few of the many faces of America were reflected in the school population of Garfield Elementary, these few faces made a difference. The black students, many of whom may have known only others of their kind, were introduced to children who were from countries few had ever heard of.

These white students knew why they were attending school. They came to school to listen and to learn. Some of these attitudes rubbed off on the black students. After the race riot in 1943 and as they approached early teen years, many of these non-black students left Garfield to attend non-secular schools. When the time came to enter Garfield Intermediate School, the entering classes were almost entirely black.

The Garfield Intermediate School

Prior to 1930, Garfield School had been a K through 8th grade elementary school. On September 1930, Garfield was reorganized into an elementary school and an intermediate school. The 1923 addition to the school site was used to house the newly designated intermediate school. Garfield Intermediate was the only intermediate school on

51

the Near Eastside. The population increase in the area had caused serious overcrowding in the upper grades of the elementary schools in the area. Garfield Intermediate was expected to take the pressure off of these classes in the neighboring schools.

The teachers at Garfield Intermediate have consistently been described as dedicated instructors who were interested, not only in imparting knowledge to the students, but in reaching and teaching the "whole person." Each student had a favorite teacher that he or she remembers fondly, but some of the teachers are spoken of consistently and reverently as truly outstanding in their contributions to the lives of the students. One such teacher was Mrs. Maxine Routt, the General Science teacher. About her is said, "She taught me about self respect and respect for

Mr. Harrison Principal & Social Studies Teacher — Garfield School.

Mrs. Junetta Watt, Beloved Home Economics Teacher, Garfield School.

others. Mrs. Routt taught me to love myself and to demonstrate this love of self through my behavior with others." A former student spoke of Mr. Harold Harrison, Social Studies teacher, as a "strong father figure, stern but enthusiastic about his subject matter." Another says of Mr. Harrison, "He had a profound effect on my intermediate school education. At all times, Mr. Harrison insisted on academic excellence." Others remember Mr. Harrison as the owner of "The Board of Education," a wooden paddle that he owned and was rumored to wield on occasion. There seems to be no female student that attended Garfield Intermediate during the years Mrs. Junetta Watts was teaching homemaking who was not influenced and inspired by her gentle, yet firm lessons on how to live one's life gracefully, graciously and fully. She taught by example how to behave as ladies and gentlemen in adult life.

As students are inspired and influenced by teachers, students unknowingly, often make a positive impact on the lives of teachers. One such teacher may well be Mr. Norm Reckling,

Northeastern High School

Northeastern High School

Northeastern High School, located on Hancock and Grandy, was opened on 1916. At the time Northeastern was built, it served the pupils of northeast Detroit to the city limits of that time. The neighborhood was then and continued to be for decades, primarily a Polish one. Because there was no high school other than Miller nearby, many black students from the Near Eastside attended Northeastern for their high school education. As the demographics changed, Northeastern became more reflective of the growing black population. Depending on when you entered Northeastern, you may have had a black teacher, though this was a rarity for those who entered high school in the 1940's.

Wood Shop teacher. Joynal Muthleb tells of encountering Mr. Reckling at Wayne State University years after leaving Garfield. Muthleb says of this meeting, "I reintroduced myself to him and as I told him about the positive influence he had on my life, I distinctly remember seeing the tears flowing down his cheek." It is probable that Mr. Reckling found much to admire and to learn from in the excellent and dedicated student Muthleb had been. Muthleb credits Mr. Norm Reckling as having a positive influence on his life. Muthleb says, " He taught me much more than the basic use of tools. Mr. Reckling involved me in an after-school Boy Scout Troop. In great measure, due to his influence, I left the Garfield School with many positive manual and academic skills."

There seems to be no consensus regarding Northeastern high school and how well it served the black students. All seem to agree that it was no panacea for black students. Some black students felt that they were denigrated and that their intellectual abilities were not being appreciated. Others felt that they were not welcome to participate in the extra curricular activities that existed at that time. These are the students that early on, made the decision to transfer to other high schools. There are some other students who can truly say that the successes they achieved in their adult life began and/or were nurtured at Northeastern High School. Notable among this group is Council Cargle whose serious interest in an acting career was sharpened as he starred in the senior play, "Father of the Bride." The outstanding basketball careers of the legendary Ernest Wagner and of John Kline, Ph.D. began on the basketball court as

(Above) Northeastern High School Cheerleaders. (Below) Class at Northeastern High School.

members of Northeastern High School's basketball team.

There were other black students who made an indelible mark in sports at Northeastern. Then there was Robert Boyce, highly successful in sports and in academia, he made "All City" in football, basketball and track Over time, the team sports at Northeastern began to lose their Polish flavor as the black athletes dominated them increasingly.

Northeastern was designed to accommodate the industrial community that surrounded it. Although it had a college prep program, the emphasis was on the technical, general and commercial programs. At times, Northeastern was a primary site for apprentice training programs for industry. Auto mechanics, vocational mathematics and machine shop were an important part of the school curriculum. Without black counselors, there was little recognition of the intellectual gifts of the black students, hence little encouragement for those who were college bound. Not surprisingly, dreams were deferred and dreams were denied for many. Yet, in the words of Maya Angelou, "And still I rise," rise we did, in our attempt to be all that we could be. Black athletes who attended Northeastern High School won many scholarships to Michigan colleges and universities.

St. Peter Claver and Sacred Heart School

In September 1936, St. Peter Claver opened the first Catholic School in Detroit specifically for Black Children. There were two classrooms with two Felician Sisters as teachers and sixty-four students. The church and school population grew steadily. As St. Peter Claver parish grew, the decision was made by the Archdiocese of Detroit to relocate the parish to Sacred Heart Church. The declining German population in the area made Sacred Heart Church available.

Sacred Heart School opened and was staffed by fifteen Felician Sisters. The first freshman class began in September 1941. The first Sacred Heart High School students received their diplomas

Holy Rosary, Tenth Grade Class (1948) Courtesy of Adrienne Lasuse.

Sacred Heart Cheerleaders (Courtesy of Jean Everage).

in June, 1945. On that day of commencement, forty-five young people graduated. When Sacred Heart School closed in June 1957 due to declining enrollment, Sacred Heart School had established a reputation for high academic standards.

The University of Islam

Detroit's newly formed Nation of Islam established the University of Islam in 1934, their own private institution. Thier school was located at 3408 Hastings Street. The school had 13 teachers including Mary Almanza, founding teacher in the Muslim Girls Training Corps where young women were trained in nursing, cooking and child rearing. Mrs. Almanza is reputed to be the original maker of the famous bean pies that have become a staple in the Nation of Islam's Black Muslim community.

On April 17, 1934, the University of Islam was raided by a squad of policemen. The teachers were arrested and booked for contributing to the delinquency of minors. Telephone wires were cut. Despite their over-kill tactics, the raid netted only two children of the more than 400 children that records indicate were enrolled there.

Following the jailing of the teachers, there was a demonstration at Detroit Police headquarters culminating in a small riot.

Most of us never return to visit the schools of our youth, but we remember....

We remember....

DETROIT PUBLIC SCHOOLS

Students of Sacred Heart School on Eliot at Rivard (circa 1946).

Joseph Love, 1946, Courtesy of Jean Everage.

Colored Mission To Open School
St. Peter Claver's to Have First Grades Next September (from Detroit Times)

A school for St. Peter –Claver Colored Mission, Eliot and Beaubien streets, will be opened next September by order of Bishop Michael J. Gallagher. The Rev. Henry P. Thiefels, C. S. Sp., the pastor, announced Wednesday that the school will open with the first and second grades in the apartment house across from the church.

It has been the wish of the bishop for a long time to have a school in this mission, but financial difficulties prevented its realization. Through the cooperation of the Felician sisters the school can now be opened. The sisters teaching in the school will reside at the motherhouse on St. Aubin avenue, and for the present the parish will not have to provide a convent for them.

St. Peter Claver parish was founded in 1911 by the Rev. Joseph Wuest, C. S. Sp., then pastor of St. Mary's church (downtown). Another parish fro colored Catholics is St Benedict the Moor, Beechwood near Warren, founded some years ago. Its pastor is the Rev. Charles Kapp, C. S. Sp..

These two parishes are real home mission works and offer opportunity for concrete practical Catholic Action now that the bishop has directed the establishment of a school for St. Peter Claver's.

Nov 28, 1936

_____

BALCH SCHOOL TURNS OUT FOR ITS ACE HERO

It was "hero's day" last Wednesday at Balch elementary school, St. Antoine and Palmer, and the faculty and student body turned out in all their pride.

Although the hero — Joseph Love-was only 13 years of age, he couldn't have been tendered a warmer reception had he been a Congressional Medal of Honor winner.

Joseph, who is a Balch school patrol boy, as well as a member of Boy Scout Troop No. 28, was accorded guest of honor spot on a special broadcast from the Balch assembly hall of Radio Station WWJ's "Safety Show," for his heroic rescue of a girl schoolmate from the path of a speeding car on Nov. 12.

Climaxing the broadcast was the presentation by Paul Williams and Fran Harris, directors of the program, of the show's "First in Safety" award to the young patrol boy.

Also featured on the show were Melvin Bates, captain of the Balch Safety Patrol and 10 first and second graders, five girls and five boys, participating in the Safety Show's "Pee-Wee Patrol Quiz," which the girls won.

————

Dorothy Greenfield

Larry Rogers, Northeastern HS, 1954.

William Wesley Edmonson, Northeastern HS, 1949.

58

Era Irving, Northeastern HS, 1950.

Louise Williams, Northeastern HS.

Frusetta Walker Clark, Northeastern HS, 1937.

Erma Harris Zackery, Cass Tech HS, 1956.

CURTAIN GOING UP!!!

Stage Crew   Northeastern Drama Club

BOTTOM: *J. Jackson, J. Stuckey, D. Stanton, E. Graves, Mr. Tokar.*
ROW II: *M. Dennard, A. Curtis, H. Oliver, W. Reed.*
ROW III: *D. Sherman.*

BOTTOM: *Elizabeth Sims, Betty Davis, Mary James, Lillian Gillum, Joyce Humphreys, Eleanor Steinhebel, Justeen Robinson, Rosemary Johnson.* ROW II: *Miss Cover, Margaret Regular, Ella Fears, Barbara Bryant, Betty Sox, Concetta Fricia, Gail Lester, Judy Manning, Mary Hawkins.* ROW III: *Helen Balash, Bobbie Guyton, Sophie Dowhan, Maytroit Slater, Arieathier Payne, Margie Mann, Wilma Parker, Shirley Battles, Susie Miles, Laverne Paige.* ROW IV: *Inez Jones, Delois Graham, Elbert Clark, Adrienne Barker, Alma Carter, Thompson Correthers, Morgan Carroll.* ROW V: *Council Cargle, Benjamin Monroe, Alfred Thacker, Edward Williams, Earlie Black, Marietta Burroughs, Anna Jean Clay, Clifford Frazier.* ROW VI: *Marion Sokolowski and Jim Mitchell.*

CHAPTER FOUR

A Profile of Some Churches on Detroit's Near East Side and Their Impact on Black Detroiters

In his book, "The Black Church in the African-American Experience," C. Eric Lincoln speaks of the Black Church as the "cultural womb of the black community," giving birth to new institutions as schools, universities, banks, credit unions, insurance companies and low income housing. From our own experience, we have seen how the Black Church has nurtured and continues to nurture musical, artistic and dramatic development in the young. We know that the Black Church has provided much more than religious teachings. It has been at the forefront of political leadership and concerns of morality. Black America's views regarding marriage, child rearing, and divorce were and continue to be shaped by the teachings of the Black Church.

At one time, church was paramount in the lives of the vast majority of black people It seemed that every family had a "church home." It was not uncommon to hear the word, "heathen," in reference to those few who could not or did not claim religious ties to a "Christian" establishment. It would have been hard to envision "Mother's Day" without seeing members of the community dressed in their finest and attending church on that Sunday wearing proudly or sadly, a white flower or a red flower on their lapels. What person living at that time can forget how the minister could elicit raw and deep emotion by speaking of a Mother's love? Could there have been a *real* Easter Sunday without the family dressing up in their Easter finery and attending church? A family was considered poor indeed who did not have "Sunday go to meeting clothes." No person in the community was more respected, even revered than *The Reverend* or *The Minister.*

As many freed slaves headed north after emancipation seeking a better life than they could achieve in the south, it was not by chance that the Near Eastside of Detroit was one of the urban areas where many of these Black Americans came to settle. At the time of emancipation, there was already a sizeable black population in Detroit, primarily on what is now the Near Eastside. Many runaway slaves had moved to the area via the Underground Railroad that had existed in border towns in Michigan and Ohio. While both black and non-black churches were deeply involved in this process, no church was more active or more regaled than was Second Baptist in Detroit. A non-black church, First Congregational, was also deeply rooted in the abolitionist movement. This church was located at the foot of Wayne and Fort Streets. The basement of their church was used to hide refugees of the Underground Railroad on their way to boats at the foot of Wayne Street. Today, the church is located at the corner of Forest and Woodward Avenue and houses the First Congregational Living Museum Underground Railroad, a museum that is open to the public.

Second Baptist, founded in 1836 and Bethel African Methodist Episcopal Church, founded in 1839 were the first two documented African-American churches in Detroit. Although these two were at the forefront of the Black Church in Detroit, there were many other churches that left their religious marks on the early African-American settlers in Detroit. The following pages give brief historical summaries and contributions of some of the many Near Eastside churches that have played and continue to play a major role in the lives of black Americans in Detroit.

Warren Ave. Baptist Church
1036 Warren at Rivard

Second Baptist Church, Detroit, Michigan

Second Baptist is legendary as the oldest Black Church in Michigan. It was founded in 1836 when thirteen former slaves broke with First Baptist of Detroit over the issue of paying dues to a church which would not let Blacks vote on church matters. Second Baptist has a long and stable history as the oldest Black Church that continues to serve downtown Detroit. Second Baptist has been blessed with visionary and capable pastors from its inception. These pastors saw as their mission, to go beyond the spiritual needs of the congregation, extending their efforts to secure economic, political and social freedom and equality for black people.

In the nineteenth century, Second Baptist served as a way station on the Underground Railroad. Frederick Douglas and John Brown were among the beneficiaries of Second Baptist's largesse. The role of Second Baptist as a station on the Underground Railroad is evidenced by the existence of basement rooms that were reserved to hide fugitive slaves. It has been estimated that Second Baptist aided four to five thousand slaves to gain their freedom. The churches pastors served as stationmasters and a church member, George De Baptiste, provided ferry service to Windsor, Canada hence to freedom. It is said that Second Baptist member, William Webb, hosted a meeting with Frederick Douglas, John Brown, De Baptiste and others to plan for the emancipation of slaves shortly before John Brown's raid on Harper's Ferry.

In 1910, when Robert L. Bradby became pastor of Second Baptist Church, the itinerant minister was commonplace. Luckily for Second Baptist, The Reverend Bradby remained pastor until his sudden death in 1946. He had a missionary zeal to work among the sick, the poor, and the unemployed. Bradby was equally committed to preserving Second Baptist as the downtown haven for the established blacks and the new migrants. Bradby is reputed to have a rapport with Henry Ford that allowed him to not only refer job seekers to the Ford plants, but to secure them jobs. Bradby's ability to link men with jobs made Second Baptist a very important church. Under Reverend Bradby, the congregation skyrocketed from the low hundreds to 3000 by 1930.

Reverend A.A. Banks was the minister who succeeded Reverend Bradby. Banks' strong organizational skills, coupled with the new wave of black migration that followed World War 11 accounted for the continued growth of Second Baptist to a peak congregation of 4800 members.

2nd Baptist Church

Bethel A.M.E. Church, Detroit

In 1839, 50 black citizens of Detroit met together and formed The Colored Methodist Society. This same group decided to associate with African Methodism. On May 10, 1841, the congregation organized itself as Bethel African Episcopal Church. It wasn't until 1849 that the church was formally incorporated. The first meetings were held in Old Military Hall, which was loaned to the society by the Detroit Common Council. Later Bethel built its first church, a brick building located on the south side of Lafayette Street just behind the Old Military Hall. This church building was dedicated on September 19, 1847.

In the late 1880's, the congregation, led by the Reverend James Henderson, raised money and built a second Bethel A.M.E. Church on the corner of Napoleon and Hastings Streets. The cost of Construction was $21,000. The cornerstone for this building was laid on December 22, 1889. A third church was build under the leadership of Reverend Joseph Gomez, pastor from 1919-1927. The site was at the corner of Frederick and St. Antoine. Bethel also bought the adjoining two family brick house to be used as the parsonage. This edifice was completed and dedicated on June 7, 1925. It was to be the home of Bethel until 1974 when under the ministry of Reverend Maurice Higginbothan, the church relocated to a three and one-half parcel of land on Warren Avenue, bounded by St. Antoine street on the west and the I-75 Service Drive on the east. This structure was built at a cost of $1,500,000 to complete and was dedicated on December 1974.

From Bethel's beginning, Missions and service to the community have been of prime importance to the church. On November 2, 1871, Reverend G.C. Booth, pastor of Bethel, along with a group of its members, organized a Mission and a Sunday school and named it Ebenezer. This is how the still thriving Ebenezer A.M.E. was begun. Another pastor, Reverend J. P. Q. Wallace established a Social Service Department in

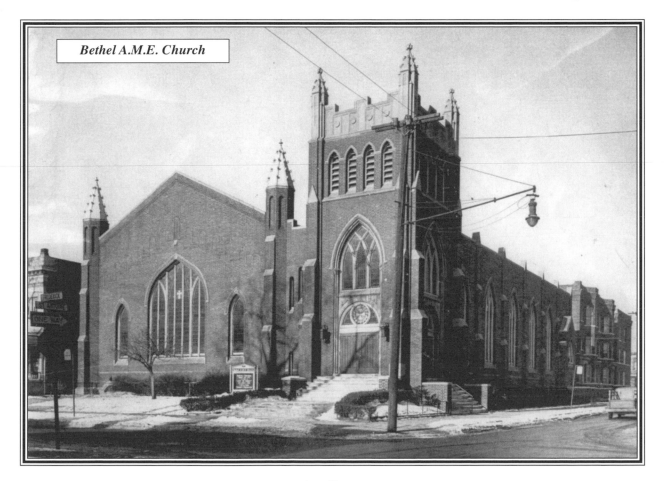

Bethel A.M.E. Church

4th Row (Top): Unk, Robert Wilson, Robert Boyce, Robert Gragg, Clauzell Saterwhite & Marvin Rogers

3rd Row: Unk, Joan Boswell, Lydia Boyce Yvonne Rogers, Unk, Unk, Unk.

2nd Row: Edward Tisdale, Unk, Justine Rogers, Unk, Unk, Unk, Dr. Lockett (Musical Director).

1st Row (Bottom): Mary Tisdale, Artheree Jeter, Unk, William Hines (Choir Director), Marilyn Bowman, Roberta Washington, & Unk.

Bethel A.M.E. Church Youth Choir

64

HOUSEWIVES' LEAGUE

Seated—Left to Right: Ethel Hemsley, Parliamentarian; Manie Boone, Chr. Organizing Com.; Mary L. Beasley, 2nd. Vice-Pres.; Nannie E. Black, 1st. Vice-Pres.; Christine Fuqua, President; Fannie B. Peck, President Emeritus; Wilha Woodford, Mrs. Baldwin, Pearl Garvin, Supervisor, Gertrude Tolbert, Secretary of Executive Board; Lila Stewart.

CHILDREN'S CHOIR

First Row—Seated: Mrs. M. E. Foster, Supervisor; Mrs. Carrie Thompson, Founder.

First Row—Standing: Davie Wright, Mary Weston, Thomas Lovejoy, Christine Grady, Morris Reddick, Charles Henry, Queen Esther Morrell, Kenneth Grady, Doris Long, Charles Madden.

Second Row: Horace Colquitt, Juanita Cavett, Sadie Weston, Edward Shaw, E. J. Nichols, John McCrae, Charles McCrae, Wm. Edmondson, Lois Benton, Charles Edmondson, Eugene Elsie, Alex. Bracken, Vernon Weston, Mitchell Maples, Alex. McDonald, Mona Mae Reddick, Barbara Windham, Juanita Smith.

Third Row—Standing: Jacqulyn P. Cushing, Robert Henry, James Tard, Charles Reddick, Cyrus Cassells, Doris Long, Edward Kirkland, Delores Irvin, James Morrell, Diana Irvin.

Fourth Row: Benjamin Hayes, Alice McCrae, Lenora Lewis, James Henry, Roberta Washington, Alice Dudley, Bernice Lyerson, Gloria Irvin, Arthur Anderson, Joseph Smith, Alvin Cain.

October, 1911. This developed into an agency for helping new emigrants to Michigan find jobs and housing.

Reverend William H. Peck, who began his dynamic ministry of Bethel in 1928, conceived the idea of **The Booker T. Washington Trade Association.** Mrs. Fannie B. Peck was instrumental in founding **The Detroit Housewives League.** These organizations were founded to assist struggling black businesses that found the Depression made it difficult to survive. Mrs. Peck also conceived and organized **The Fannie B. Peck Credit Union.** It was the first black credit union in the United States to receive a state charter.

The Bethel Benefit Association was formed as a way for the membership to better themselves economically. This association was an insurance, which charged a fee of fifty cents to join and twenty-five cents a month premium. It paid three dollars a week for up to six weeks in a calendar year and paid seventy-five dollars death benefit.

Today, Bethel A.M.E. Church, through the **Bethel Non Profit Housing** Corporation, has spearheaded the development of a modern 120 one-bedroom apartment building and 26 two- and three-bedroom townhouses. Bethel A.M.E. continues to be deeply involved in the community and is one of the catalysts for the development of housing in the Medical Center Community.

Plymouth Congregational Church at Beaubien & Garfield

Prior to *1927,* the Church Home for Plymouth had been at St. Aubin and Antietam. For a short period, Plymouth Church had held services in the Fellowship Hall of First Congregational Church and later in the Masonic Temple.

Rev. Laviscount, pastor of Plymouth 1924-26, discovered the building that became Plymouth Congregational Church on a walking tour in the vicinity. It had been a Jewish Synagogue before the congregation purchased it in 1927 at a cost of $55,000. The building was only nine years old at the time of its purchase, constructed of solid brick and concrete and furnished in oak. It had an auditorium that seated 600 and a full basement that

This Certifies That on the first day of April, in the year 1934 Lienora Lewis received Christian Baptism in Bethel A.M.E Church at Detroit State of Michigan Wm H. Peck Minist.

THE FUTURE HOME OF THE PLYMOUTH CONGREGATIONAL CHURCH
Garfield at Beaubien, Detroit, Michigan
The above building was a Jewish Temple until November 1, when it was purchased by the Plymouth Congregational Church.
The construction is solid brick and concrete. It is beautifully finished and furnished in oak. The Auditorium seats 600. There is a full basement that will seat 300, with ample kitchen and other rooms. The building was constructed nine years ago and cost $87,000 without furnishings. The land value alone has just been appraised at $32,000.

Financial Statement

The purchase price of the entire property		$55,000
Down payment by Plymouth Church $ 5,000		
Pledged Grant and Loan from the Congregational Church Building Society, New York	10,000	
Pledged Loan, Detroit Cong'l Union	5,000	
Total loans and gifts to date	$20,000	20,000
Amount to be secured in this campaign		$35,000

Campaign Begins Nov. 21 and Ends Dec. 5

Plymouth Congregational Church at Beaubien & Garfield

could seat 300. The church was complete with an ample kitchen and other amenities. Plymouth Church remained in that building for 47 years.

Reverend Horace White assumed the pastorate of the church in 1936. Rev. White was an activist who instilled new hope and activity in the church. He increased the membership and purchased a new pipe organ. Rev. White had a weekly radio broadcast and wrote a weekly column for the Michigan Chronicle newspaper. Three ministers were ordained under his leadership including the Rev. AIbert Cleage. After Rev. White's death in 1958, the Reverend Nicholas Hood, II, a graduate from Yale Divinity School, became the Senior Minister of Plymouth. Rev. Hood was Senior Minister from 1958-1985.

PIymouth Congregationd Church had a profound and positive influence on the teen-agers in the 1940's and 1950's. It provided a place popularly called a canteen where the young people could meet and sociaiize in a proper manner, chaperoned, of course. This canteen was so popular, it beckoned teens from all over the city to mix and mingle. The auditorium provided an arena in which plays and other events were stagcd.

The new Plymouth Church was constructed in 1974. PIymouth Church was one of the first churches in America to construct housing for low-income families. Under the leadership of Rev. Nicholas Hood, Sr., 42 acres of new apartments, senior citizens apartments and housing were constructed for low and moderate-income families. Special housing was built for mentally retarded citizens. Every contractor was black except for the heating and plumbing contractor.

Ebenezer African Methodist Episcopal Church

Ebenezer African Methodist Church began in Cook's Hall, on the corner of Prospect and Watson. Rev. G.C. Booth was the pastor. It was organized as a Mission and a Sunday School under the guidance of Reverend G.C. Booth of Bethel A.M.E. and a group of its members. Ebenezer, mcaning "stone of help," was to serve as a refuge for freedom seeking worshippers. On November 2, 1871, Ebenezer moved into a new church home located on Calhoun Street. This new church became the first church sanctuary. Under the pastorate of Reverend C.H. Ward, a second church was purchased on Erskine Street and the first church was made into the parsonage.

Ebenezer had been organized for a two-fold purpose, first, to worship and to provide spiritual uplift, and second, to serve as a civic center for the people of the community. As a part of its community effort, Ebenezer organized the first Cradle Society for mothers who brought their babies to be blessed. Later, this project became a day nursery.

An event of historical significance took place under the pastorate of Reverend C.E. Allen. Henry Ford was, at that time, a struggling inventor who needed help to get his invention started. Mr. Ford came to the parsonage of Ebenezer and requested and received contributions from the congregation to help finance his company's experiments. In appreciation, Henry Ford, though still a poor man in the 1900's, sent donations to Ebenezer which far exceeded the collections he received from the members. The personal letters of gratitude from Mr. Ford remain priceless possessions of the Allen Family.

The Reverend G.W. Baber was assigned to Ebenezer in 1933. Under his leadership, Ebenezer experienced its greatest growth. On December 22, 1935, the third church home was purchased. This church, described as a magnificent temple, was located at the corner of Willis and Brush Streets. Ebenezer attracted members from the entire Detroit community. With a congregation exceeding 3000, Ebenezer quickly

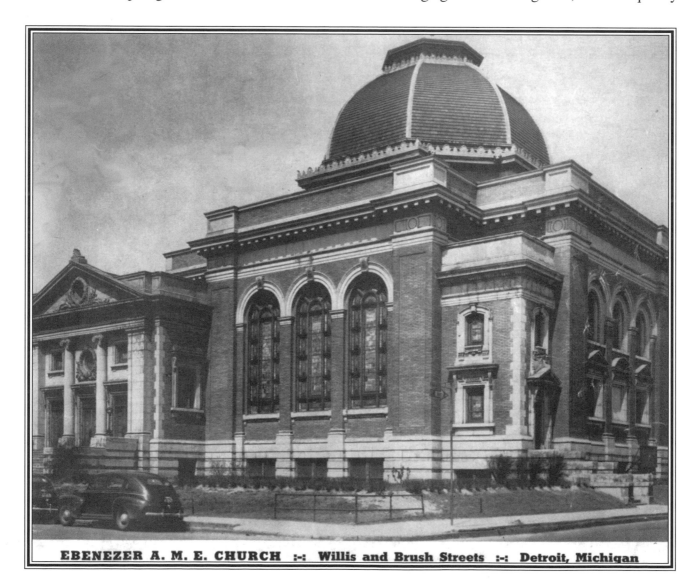

EBENEZER A. M. E. CHURCH :-: Willis and Brush Streets :-: Detroit, Michigan

GIRL SCOUTS TROOP NO. 247

First Row—Janice Moore. *Second Row*—Gwendolyn Walters, Dorothy Overall, Jane Ann Bass. *Third Row*—Corrine Gillespie, Delores Ramsey, Louise Jones, Patricia Pierce, Helen Lee, Marion Webb. *Fourth Row*—Anna L. Adkins, Julia Thornton, Jessie Burke, Lottie Brazelton, Margaret Overall, **Rosalind Nattee.** *Fifth Row*—**Constance Bodley, Angeline Evans, Dorothy Gillespie, Anna M. Bryant, Gloria Garrett, Anna L. Lundy.** *Sixth Row*—Catherine Freeman, Delores Garrett, Audrey Marshall, Alice Rogers. *Seventh Row*—Esther Kelsaw, Lillian Miller, Maudess Williams. *Back Row*—Mrs. Billie Witt, Mrs. Josephine Jones, Leader, Mrs. Fannie Pierce, Asst. Leader.

A corner of the gymnasium of Ebenezer Church which is used as a Dormitory for soldiers, sailors, and marines. One hundred double-deck beds are available. The ladies of the USO and Ebenezer Church cooperate in maintaining the Dormitory.

LADIES' USHER BOARD

First Row—Diane Peeples, Henrietta Carr, Jessie M. Moody, Jean McCann, Mrs. Baber, Esther Hickman, President, Rev. Baber, Helen Lewis, Louise Brown, Anna Cager, Lillie Brown. *Second Row*—Mary Harbin, Ella Ballinger, Virginia Jackson, Annie F. Simmons, Sadie Mickle, Ophelia Foster, Henrietta Foster, Emma Smith, Minnie Bennett, Hattie Oneal, Beatrice Littlejohn, C. M. Castleberry. *Third Row*—Ora Jackson, Zelma Meadows, Addie Tinsley, Ethel Ivy, Anna Powell, Evelyn Branch, Ardelia, Jones, Bessie Bryant. *Fourth Row*—V. McLaughlin, Leila Wiggin, Emmie Goolsby, Lillie Holsey, Blanche Roundtree. *Fifth Row*—Sallie Fernandis, R. L. Williams, Juanita Martin, Ludie Hill, Lula Danley, Pearl Crayton.

MEN'S USHER BOARD

First Row—C. Brown, Robt. Harris, Russell Cave, R. Meadows, J. P. Brown, Vice-Pres., Lewis Smith, President, Leo Peeples, O. H. Ballinger. *Second Row*—Wm. Carter, Chas. C. Bryant, V. S. Burke, E. Crawford, Petris Davis. *Third Row* — Alex Riddick, Chas. Mickle, J. H. Woodson, Jeff Lewis, J. B. George, J. Dillard, W. Manning, W. Ross.

EBENEZER AFRICAN METHODIST EPISCOPAL CHURCH

became one of the focal points of the black community. Ebenezer's gymnasium served as a recreation and training facility for the community. During World War II, the church gymnasium, where Joe Louis once trained, was used as a dormitory to house hundreds of soldiers through cooperation with the USO.

In 1960, a fire forced Ebenezer to find a new home. The congregation worshiped temporarily at City Temple Seventh Day Adventist Church, then back to its small chapel in 1961. On July 12,1964, Reverend Hubert Robinson led Ebenezer into its fourth and present home on West Chicago Boulevard.

––––––––

New Bethel Baptist Church

Long before the Reverend C.L. Franklin put his mark on New Bethel Baptist Church, it was a church of prominence in the black community and one of the most important. It was located on Hastings Street at Willis Street on the Near Eastside. New Bethel was a large church by yesterday's standards. It was beautiful! The pews were of solid and highly polished oak. The altar was large and impressive, with ample room for the presiding minister, the assistant ministers and many of the visiting dignitaries.

On Baptismal Sundays, there was a large pool for the immersion ceremony. It stood in front on the left side of the alter. Women, referred to as nurses, wore crisp white uniforms and nurse's hats. These nurses were there to comfort the churchgoers, fanning them and returning those who "became happy" back to their pews. These nurses were a calming influence for the occasions when the preacher's sermon raised the tensions of the worshippers dramatically.

The Sunday School classes at New Bethel were popular. Children came from miles around to attend. The Sunday School lessons were printed on colorful brochures that were collected at the end of class for later reuse. The emphases of the lessons were on stories from the Old Testament.

Perhaps because they were more graphic, they may have been more interesting for children than some of the stories from the New Testament. The lessons were broken down into several classes according to age. In addition to the stories from the Bible, Negro spirituals and hymns were taught as well as inspirational poetry and mini plays. Every Sunday school attendee was encouraged to learn a poem, sing a song, or give a small speech for Children's Day Sunday.

It wasn't until the Reverend C.L. Franklin assumed the ministry at New Bethel Baptist Church in 1946 that the church became of note nationwide. Franklin was a gifted and charismatic orator. Flamboyant and controversial, Franklin's skills as a speaker/preacher drew followers from around the country, drawn by his dynamic and eloquently soulful preaching style. Reverend Franklin, the  father of the famed singer, Aretha Franklin, was also an important and respected political figure. It was Franklin who organized the Walk to Freedom Civil Rights March in Detroit in June 1963 where Martin Luther King delivered for the first time, a version of his famous "I Have a Dream" speech. For more than 30 years, Reverend Franklin's sermons were broadcast on Detroit radio station WJLB.

Today, New Bethel Baptist Church is located at 8450 C.L. Franklin Boulevard.

––––––––

71

St. Peter Claver Church

St. Peter Claver Roman Catholic Church was founded in 1911 to take care of the many colored Catholics who lived on the East Side of Detroit. It was founded by the Rev. Joseph Wuest, C.S. Sp. At that time, Wuest was the pastor of St. Mary's Church in downtown Detroit. The parish was placed in charge of the Holy Ghost Fathers. The church was named for St. Peter Claver, a Jesuit priest from Spain. Claver moved to the new world as a young man in 1610 and for 44 years ministered to African slaves in South America. St. Peter Claver not only ministered to and interceded for the slaves, but made many attempts to stop the slave trade. During his life, St. Peter Claver is said to have instructed and baptized more than 300,000 Negro slaves. On July 7, 1896, St. Peter Claver was named special patron of all Negro Catholic missions. He died in 1654 in Cartagena.

St. Peter Claver Church was located on Eliot and Beaubien streets. The parish has been described as a "home mission parish" that offered opportunities for concrete practical Catholic action. By their 25th anniversary in 1936, the church was able to realize a long cherished dream to open a grade school, the first Catholic school for colored children in the city of Detroit. This was a massive undertaking for such a small parish, but under the guidance of The Rev. Henry P. Thiefels, C.S. Sp., and through many fund-raising activities and benefits, enough funding was achieved for the school to open.

————

September 1, 1911
Old St. Mary's School
Beginning of St. Peter Claver

1914 November
† Happy Thanksgivin
A new worship site
is purchased,
and the first
Mass is
celebrated

September 1, 1938
Great celebration — March from Eliot and Beaubien to our new and current home, SACRED HEART

Sacred Heart Church

Although Detroit was a multi-ethnic community in the nineteenth century, each ethnic group clung to its own religious life. The various ethnic communities built their own churches so that they could express their religion according to their own customs. In 1875, a group of German-American Catholics established Sacred Heart Church at what is now Eliot and Rivard. They were also given permission to establish a school.

Racism and segregation prevented Black Catholics from being accepted in most Catholic congregations. On September 1, 1911, eighteen Black Catholics met with Fr. Joseph Wuest, C.S.Sp., pastor of Old St. Mary's. With his assistance, a large classroom was made available. This classroom served as a chapel for Black Catholics for three years.

By 1914, the congregation had outgrown their chapel. They purchased a small Episcopal Church located on Beaubien Streets. The new parish was named St. Peter Claver for the man who was canonized in 1851 as the Universal Patron of Missions to Black people. This church was a joyful place of worship and for other activities. The many dances, picnics, club meetings and choir practices and other social involvements gave rise to increased concerns for the larger society and highlighted the need for political participation.

Father Charles Kapp, C.S. Sp. pastored the parish for eight years. When Father Henry Thiefels, C.S. Sp. became pastor in 1932, the rectory was remodeled to provide two classrooms.

As the number of Black Catholics increased, negotiations began with the Archdiocese of Detroit to relocate the parish at Sacred Heart Church. On September 1, 1938 the parishioners of St. Peter Claver marched in procession up Eliot Street, across Hastings to Rivard and celebrated Mass in their new church.

With the urban removal that was the result of replacing a still vibrant Hastings Street with the Chrysler Freeway, many families moved away joining other parishes, their children attending different schools. The numbers have diminished, yet devoted and determined parishioners remain. You can find Sacred Heart Church in the historic Eastern Market District. The Sacred Heart Parish has seen a recent increase to over 1300 families or 3500 individuals. The Sacred Heart Activities Building, erected in 1980, has been enlarged twice to accommodate the many celebrations, activities and organizations.

————

St. Paul African Methodist Episcopal Zion Church

St. Paul A.M.E. Zion Church began in the Catherine Street home of Mr. C. C. Cox in 1911. The first pastor was the Rev. James Terry. In 1922, Rev. I.Q. Conquest became the pastor. At that time, worship services were held temporarily in the old Vaudeville Theater on Gratiot Street when the Catherine Street structure was destroyed.

In 1922, Rev. P. R. Flack became the pastor and led the congregation in the purchase of a church at 521 E. Palmer.

In 1941, under the stewardship of Rev. Lott P. Powell, scholarships to Livingston College in North Carolina were established.

Rev. William Alexander Hilliard assumed pastoral leadership of St. Paul from 1947-1960 when the congregation moved to their present location on Dexter Avenue in Detroit. Under his leadership, Rev. Hilliard established a Sunday nursery for the children and oversaw the move to the Dexter Avenue facility. In 1960, Rev. Hilliard became the 67th Bishop in succession of the African Methodist Episcopal Zion Church.

————

St. Paul A. M. E. Parsonage

An Evening Extravaganza at St. Paul A.M.E. Zion Church (521 E. Palmer Street) — "KING SOLOMAN'S WEDDING." Seated right of King Soloman & His Queen are Louis Mitchell, Jr. (a Royal Guard) and Rev. and Mrs. L. P. Powell,

Ladies Aide, St. Paul A.M.E. Zion Church

PROPHET JONES AND HIS CHURCH OF UNIVERSAL TRIUMPH, THE DOMINION OF GOD, INC.

James Francis Marion Jones, AKA Prophet Jones, was perhaps the most flamboyant and colorful religious leader in Detroit in the 1940's and 50's. Reverend James F. Jones came to Detroit from Birmingham, Alabama in 1938 at the age of 21 as a missionary preacher and formed a sect called Triumph the Church and Kingdom of God in Church. His evangelistic style resonated with many converts who lavished opulent gifts upon him. Later, he broke away from this sect and founded his own church that he named "Church of Universal Triumph, the Dominion of God."

Some have said that Prophet Jones once held religious services at the old Medbury Theater on Hastings and Medbury. The old Oriole Theater at 8450 Linwood is generally recognized as his first church. He later moved to the Fine Arts Theater at 2940 Woodward. Prophet Jones' Detroit membership was approximately 1500. The reach of his radio voice is not known, but the Prophet claimed six million followers nationwide.

The Prophet's church services were unique, beginning at 10 p.m.. and lasting until 7 or 8 the next morning. The Prophet himself did not appear until midnight or later, "as God ordered him to." Once he began preaching, he did not stop for five or six hours. His appearances at the services were compelling. Prophet Jones would stroll down the aisle of the church flanked by his princes and princesses, lords and ladies, and dressed in the finest silk and satin robes. He most often wore a gem-encrusted beret and an earring in his left ear only, so that his right ear was open to any messages that God desired to send him.

Jone's arrival to the church is said to make New Year's Eve celebrations pale by comparison. The choir voices would explode with hymns, accompanied by cymbals and tambourines, organ music and gut-bucket style piano. In the aisles and on the stage, voices would burst out in song and shouting. Part of his attraction was perhaps his main tenet, that all men would become immortal in 2000 A.D.; that heaven would come to earth, abolishing death and all of man's ills, if one obeyed his decrees. These decrees were primarily about health, cleanliness and morality issues, such as no illegitimate children and no drinking or smoking. These decrees dovetailed with ideas held by many people.

In the 40's Prophet Jones moved into a Mediterranean-style home at 246 Ferry with his mother, Catherine. People often gathered just to see the Prophet's appearance at his front door. He would appear adorned with one of his fabulous collection of mink coats and a king's ransom of diamond jewelry. Always surrounded by bodyguards, the Prophet had a regal persona, an imposing dignity. At his parties there, one could not speak to the Prophet except through an aide called a "linguist." He would answer only through this "linguist." In 1944, Prophet Jones sold the Ferry Street house to M. Kelly Fritz and moved to Arden Park. The Ferry Street home of the prophet became the Fritz Funeral Home. He moved to Chicago in 1956 after being arrested on a morals charge for which he was subsequently acquitted in Detroit's Recorder's Court.

Prophet James Francis Marion Jones

Reflections of Some Near EastSide Residents on Their Experiences in the Black Churches in Their Neighborhood

George D. Ramsey Sr. recalls, "Among the neighbors on the block was Reverend Matthews, the pastor of **Warren Avenue Baptist Church**, located at 1036 E. Warren at Rivard where it still stands. Reverend Matthews lived at 928 E. Warren and over the years, I witnessed his daily ritual of building on parts of his church that still stands in testimony to his workmanship as does the spiritual messages he left with me. This was the first church my Mother took me to and I attended "religiously" until I turned 12 and got my paper route. This is where I first heard my mother singing, "What a Friend We Have in Jesus," and I have loved it ever since. I have been truly blessed with music being around me most of my life, and it wasn't by accident, it was because I lived on Warren, my "Street of Dreams."

Era J. Irving Williamson in recounting her experiences at **Bethel A.M.E. Church** writes, "Although I attended Mt. Olive Baptist Church, much of the time, I would go to Bethel because I could sing in the Children's Choir. At that time, the minister was Rev. Peck. His wife formed an organization known as the Housewives League, and I among others was a member of the Junior Housewives League. We met every week at a neighbor's home. There we were taught about our black history, culture and etiquette. A Mrs. Ashford taught us how to set a table correctly, how to dress properly, i.e. to keep our pants up and our skirts down and to use ladylike behaviors and speech at all times. We learned about current events and past history through reading and discussing Ebony Magazines and from the teachings of our elders."

Dorothy Greenfield Hill writes, "My spiritual background was nurtured at **Plymouth Congregational Church**, then on Garfield and Beaubien under Reverend Horace White. The old Plymouth Congregational Church is now Plymouth United Church of Christ. My minister, The Reverend Horace White was a great motivator for the community. His sermons often centered on the value of praying and working together to create a better community for the residents. Reverend White taught that with faith in God, one could achieve.

Council Cargle starred in his first theatrical performance at **Scott Methodist Episcopal Church** on St. Antoine and Kirby. His role was that of Jesus Christ in a Christmas Pageant. Council was so moved by his first acting performance; that he decided to continue in theater, becoming Detroit's premier actor.

Justine Rogers Wylie remembers **Scott Methodist Episcopal Church** as the church where many of her family were members. Scott was the largest African-American Methodist Episcopal Church in Detroit. It stood at the corner of E. Kirby and St. Antoine in a building that was a former Jewish Synagogue. She recalls the Vacation Bible School that she and other children throughout the neighborhood attended in the summer and the big church picnic that was held each year. This is the church her parents were married in and later, in their newer church on Chicago Blvd. were buried from.

Some Childhood Memories of Jean Everage "At age 6, I attended Sunday School at **St. Paul A.M.E. Zion Church** 521 E. Palmer Street. It was a weekly joy, a place of learning and a meeting place. Sunday services filled with families and relatives, adults and children, were a common sight during my childhood and early adulthood. My sister, Bernice and our mother, Julia Everage were members also. We participated in religious and social services centered on the church. In the hot summer months, open windows and sturdy cardboard fans provided the air-conditioning. When St. Paul moved to a new location in 1959, I became a charter member of **Metropolitan A.M.E. Zion** at the 521 Palmer location."

———

Holy Rosary Church, Woodward & Medbury

Dorothy Helen Wilson, Nurse at Rev. Lofton's Church, was an entrepreneur and neighborhood legend.

John & Sylvia Braithwaite 1st Communion, Sacred Heart Church, 1942.

Scott Methodist Episcopal Church, St. Antoine & Kirby.

CHAPTER FIVE
WHERE STARS WERE BORN
THE NEAR EASTSIDE CONNECTION

It is said that the most brilliant stars in the galaxy are those born closest to the Milky Way's black hole. These are the stars that burn brightest but whose lifespan is briefest. Though there is a lack of agreement about the theory of the black hole and even of its very existence, there is no doubt that on the Near Eastside of Detroit, for many years the center of the Black Community, many of Detroit's brightest stars were created. Not all of these stars were native Near Eastsiders; some were transplants. All came to achievement in a climate and at a time when life was not easy for most Americans and for relatively few Black Americans. These are the people, sung and unsung heroes, who are being highlighted in this chapter. These are the people who, when they met an obstacle, did not walk around it, but instead made the effort to push it out of the way. We salute these Doctors, Lawyers and Indian Chiefs who had the courage or vision to develop a life working paper that continues to inspire, encourage and enrich our lives.

Honorable Richard H. Austin

The Honorable Richard H. Austin made history as Michigan's 1st black Secretary of State and as the state's 1st black Certified Public Account. He was Michigan's longest serving Secretary of State, being re-elected a record breaking five times Austin was the father of the motor-voter law that partnered voter registration with driver's registration.

Austin grew up on the Near Eastside of Detroit and is reputed to have been a shoeshine boy in the late 1920s during the Great Depression. Austin was a member of Bethel A.M.E. Church. His public service career was launched when he was elected as a delegate to the Michigan Constitutional Convention in 1961. In 1966, Austin was elected Wayne County Auditor. Richard Austin was on the board of directors of The United Way Community Services, The NAACP, The YMCA and Bethel A.M.E. Church. Richard Austin died on April 20, 2001 at the age of 87.

Ralph Johnson Bunche was the first person of color anywhere in the world to be awarded the Nobel Prize for Peace. From June 1947 to August 1949, Bunche worked on the most important assignment of his career, the confrontation between Arabs and Jews in Palestine. He won the Nobel Prize for Peace in 1950 for the successful negotiation of the armistice agreement that ended the first Arab-Israeli war in 1949. He achieved this signed treaty after 11 months of virtually ceaseless negotiation as acting mediator on Palestine. Bunche was given a hero's welcome upon his return to the United States. New York city gave Bunche a ticker-tape parade up Broadway. Los Angeles proclaimed a Ralph Bunche Day. He was awarded over 30 honorary degrees in the next three years, and was awarded the Springarn Prize by the NAACP in 1949.

Ralph Bunche was born into an integrated community on the Near Eastside of Detroit on August 7, 1904. His father, Fred Bunche, was a barber; his mother, Olive Johnson Bunche, was an amateur musician. When he was ten years old, the family moved to Albuquerque, New Mexico. Both of his parents died there. At the age of thirteen, Bunche moved to Los Angeles with his two sisters where his maternal grandmother raised him. In Los Angeles, Bunche worked at odd jobs, among them, selling newspapers, and working as a houseboy for a movie actor.

. Ralph Bunche's intellectual brilliance was apparent at an early age. He won prizes in English and history in elementary school. He was valedictorian of his class at Jefferson High School, where he had been a debater and an all-around athlete, competing in football, basketball, baseball and track. He attended the University of California on an athletic scholarship, which he subsidized by working as a janitor. Active in debate and in campus journalism, Bunche graduated from the university in 1927 *summa cum laude,* valedictorian of his class, with a major in international relations.

Bunche began his graduate studies at Harvard University with a scholarship granted him by the university and with a thousand dollars raised by the black community in Los Angeles. When he completed his Master's degree in 1928, he taught at Howard University and worked toward his doctorate from Harvard, which he completed in 1934. He chaired the Department of political science at Howard University from 1928 to 1950. Bunche taught at Harvard from 1950-1952.

Bunche was always active in the civil rights movement where he was considered a young radical intellectual who criticized America's social system and the established Negro organizations. Like most black intellectuals of his time, Bunche believed that racial progress was synonymous with integration.

James Boyce

Bunch did not lead African American organizations, but supported them in their quest for integration.

James Boyce, a Near Eastsider who grew up on Kirby Street, attended Garfield Elementary and Intermediate School and was a member since childhood of Bethel A.M.E.Church is often spoken of and remembered as a high school All-American basketball player who led his Northwestern High School team to a city championship in 1954. Some others may remember James Boyce as an assistant coach at University of Detroit and the University of Michigan or as head coach at Eastern Michigan University.

Boyce played basketball for the University of Detroit, where he earned a Bachelor's degree. He became head basketball coach in the 1970's at Kettering High School in Detroit. After his stint at college coaching, Boyce returned to Detroit Public Schools as head coach at Munford High School.

As head coach at Munford, Boyce introduced ballroom dancing to gym classes. Boyce saw ballroom dancing as a multi-pronged activity, one that would foster social skills by allowing boys to touch girls in a socially acceptable way. Dancing was also part of Boyce's plan to combat obesity among youngsters and to make the heavy-set student more acceptable socially by becoming a good dancer. Boyce knew that many youngsters tried to get out of taking gym classes for such reasons as unwillingness to get their hair wet. Dancing was one of the carrots used to encourage kids to get their gym credits and participate in physical activity that did not discriminate against the overweight or the less athletic.

The program has been wildly successful. Today, middle school and high school students and their teachers at several Detroit schools are waltzing, foxtrotting, tangoing and cha-cha-chaing around gym floors as a direct result of Boyce's teachings. His efforts started a craze that has spread out into Metro Detroit society. The "James Boyce Foundation" was founded after his death in April 2001. The foundation began in 2002 with a dinner dance at the Roostertail as a fund raising effort to provide scholarships for promising dancer/students. In 2003 and 2004, having outgrown the Roostertail, the supporters of the foundation filled the large ballroom at Cobo Hall

Robert Boyce

ensuring that ballroom dancing be encouraged to continue in the Detroit Public Schools by the showcasing of dancers from the various schools and by the awarding of college scholarships to those students of promise.

Robert Boyce was one of five sons and two daughters of Dorcas and Robert Boyce. With his family, he grew up on the Near Eastside of Detroit and lived in the following locations, Russell at Farnsworth, Hendrie and Hastings and Kirby between Hastings and Rivard. Robert attended Balch Elementary, Garfield Intermediate and Northeastern High School. At Northeastern High, Robert was a phenomenal athlete, where he played basketball, football and ran track. He made All-City in all three sports. His athletic prowess won him a 4-year scholarship to Wayne University, now Wayne State. Boyce received a B.A. and M. Educ. from Wayne University.

Robert began his life's work as a teacher. As a teacher, he was awarded a Fulbright Scholarship to England in 1962. As an educator, Robert wore many hats. Boyce served as counselor in the Detroit Public Schools. He was Assistant Principal at Central High School, Principal at Murray Wright High School, Assistant Superintendent of Detroit Schools at Areas D and G in charge of all high schools. Robert was elected and served on the Detroit School Board for four years. He was elected President of the Detroit School Board at a controversial time in the Board's history.

Council Cargle is a distinguished and veteran actor whose career has spanned four decades. He has graced the stages of the Detroit Repertory Theatre, Plowshares Theatre, Attic Theatre, Harmonie House Playhouse and the Jewish Ensemble Theatre, to name a few. Council was intimately involved in Woodie King Jr.'s famous Concept East group of the '50s, also the Stables, the Phoenix, and the World Stage theatre groups and Drama Associates His co-stars and friends included names as Lily Tomlin, Ernie Hudson, Walter Mason and Max Wright. Looking back,

Council Cargle

Council says, "I have probably been with every group of any consequence in Detroit Theatre."

Cargle has played an awesome variety of roles that have earned him critical acclaim and awards. He has given dynamic dimension to leading and supportive characters in such roles as Cyphus in "Home," Troy Mason in "Fences," Seth in "Joe Turner's Come and Gone," Harry in "The Stillborn Lover," Sgt. Walters in "Soldiers Play," Midge in "I'm Not Rappaport" and in countless other roles. His acting talents have sent him to perform in an Alabama Shakespeare Festival as well as the St. Louis Black Repertory. Lawrence Devine, Free Press Theater Critic, describing Cargle as imminently gifted and trustworthy says of Cargle, "If ever a performance of Cargle's looks bad, critics don't blame him, they blame the play."

Cargle's formidable talents have earned him much critical acclaim and awards including the Lee Hills Award for distinguished career service from the Detroit Free Press, the Sankofa Award for theatre excellence from the Plowshares Theatre, and the Best Actor Award from the subscribers of the Detroit Repertory Theatre. Most recently, Cargle received the first ever E. Ray Scott Michigan Artist Prize from Artserve and won Best Actor Award for

his portrayal of Midge in "I'm Not Rappaport" from the Detroit Free Press, the Oakland Press and Between the Lines.

In addition to his many theatre credits, Cargle has performed in three feature films, "Detroit 9000" with Hari Rhodes, "Word of Honor" with Karl Malden, and a voice-over in Quentin Tarrantino's "Jackie Brown." He has recorded with Ruby Dee, an audio/book play of Ron Milner's "Checkmates" and has appeared in dozens of television commercials. A consummate professional, Cargle is a member of Actor's Equity, The Screen Actors Guild and A.F.T.R.A.

Dr. Bernadine Newsom Denning grew up on the Near Eastside of Detroit in the 1940s. She attended Garfield School and was a graduate of Northeastern High School and Wayne State University. Denning's career as an educator began when she taught swimming and fitness at the Lucy Thurman YWCA at the age of 14. She began her formal teaching career in 1951 as a classroom teacher for the Detroit Board of Education. When she retired from the Detroit School District she was Assistant Superintendent for School/Community Relations. Denning served also as Director of the Title 1V Office, Director of Urban Programs in Education, Director of Special Studies, and Assistant Professor of Education at the University of Michigan.

As Director of the Human Rights Office for the City of Detroit, Dr. Denning offered leadership

Dr. Bernadine Newsom Denning

to the civil rights movement. She was appointed by President Jimmy Carter as Director of the Office of Revenue Sharing for the U.S. Department of Treasury. Governor William Milliken appointed Dr. Denning vice -chair of the Michigan Women's commission from 1981-1987.

The YMCA is one of the many organizations to which Dr. Denning has contributed her time. She has served as YWCA of the USA Board Vice-President and Chairperson of the triennial YWCA convention. At present, Dr. Denning is a member of the Board of Trustees of the YWCA of Metropolitan Detroit.

Barry Gordy was born in Detroit and lived part of his life on the Near Eastside of Detroit where he attended Garfield School. Barry had a great interest in and love for music. He began writing songs as a teen-ager and continued into his adulthood. Barry's interests were wide ranging. He worked in the automobile industry for a while and trained to be a professional boxer for a while. After Gordy's return from New York City where he lived for a time, he founded Motown Records, which he nurtured from his home on West Grand Boulevard.

Gordy was a genius at selecting artists to showcase. Through such artists as Smokey Robinson, Marvin Gaye, Diana Ross and the Supremes and the Jackson Five, the Motown Sound became world renown and highly successful. Gordy amassed a fortune through Motown and helped many of his artists become, not only millionaires, but also world famous. Berry sold Motown in 1978 following his move to Los Angeles, California. His home, the former Motown studio is now the Motown Museum, attracting visitors from around the world.

Judge James Robert Gragg was born and lived his young life on Ferry Avenue on the Near Eastside of Detroit. Unlike most Black Americans of his time, he was born into an illustrious and prosperous family. His mother, Rosa Slade Gragg, was a social and political activist who served as president of the Detroit Association of Colored Women's Clubs before she founded the Slade-Gragg

Barry Gordy Hits Ville

Judge James Robert Gragg

Academy of Practical Arts on the southwest corner of Ferry and Brush. Gragg grew up in that large Georgian style home. He attended Balch Elementary, Garfield Intermediate and Northeastern High School. At Northeastern High School, Gragg was an outstanding athlete, winning eleven letters in sports.

Gragg received his Bachelor of Arts Degree in 1957 at Howard University and his Juries Doctorate at Wayne State University School of Law in 1962. His outstanding private practice and his work as an attorney for the Detroit public Schools and for the Model Neighborhood Inner City Drug Abuse Clinic attracted the attention of Governor Blanchard. In 1984 he was appointed Judge of the Probate Court. He served on the bench until illness prevented his continuance.

Sir Roland Hanna lived on the Near Eastside of Detroit and attended Lincoln School as a young child. One Near Eastsider remembers Hanna as being the *groom* in one of the Tom Thumb Weddings that were popular in the 1930s. Hanna was one of the last of the great piano players to come out of Detroit along with Barry Harris and Tommy Flanagan. Hanna studied music at Eastman and Julliard His style was diverse and fit easily into swing, bop and the classical music genre.

Impressed with Hanna's swinging and versatile musicianship, Benny Goodman hired him in 1958 for his orchestra. Hanna worked with Charlie Mingus in1959 but most often was the leader of his own trio. Hanna was part of the Thad Jones/Mel Lewis orchestra (1967-1974). He helped found the The New York Jazz Quartet with Frank Wess. Hanna composed many works for groups of various sizes, both jazz and classical. The Detroit Symphony performed his composition "Oasis" for piano and orchestra in 1993. Hanna was also an educator and tenured professor at Queens College in New York.

It has been said that Hanna was given Knighthood (thus the "Sir") from Queen Elizabeth, but current biographical data about Hanna reads that the President of Liberia in 1970 conferred Knighthood on Hanna in recognition of a series of concerts held to benefit Liberian children. Hanna

Bessie Louise Williams Ernst

passed away at the age of 70 on November 13, 2002.

Bessie Louise Williams Ernst was born on the near Eastside of Detroit during the days of the Great Depression. Living on Medbury Street placed her in the heart of Detroit's Cultural Center and an area known as the city's racial melting pot. She spent many hours at the main branch of the Detroit Public Library listening to stories in the Children's Room and she spent many Saturdays viewing the monthly puppet shows at the DIA. Louise believes the availability of these facilities and the determination of her parents to educate their children ignited a passion for learning that has yet to subside.

Louise attended and graduated from Wayne University with a Bachelor of Arts Degree assisted by scholarships, financial aid from her family and a part time job at the Detroit Public Library.

As an educator with the Detroit Public Schools, Louise went through the ranks as librarian, teacher, Coordinator of School Volunteers and the E.P.I.C. Program, and as Administrative Assistant for Program Development. Her final position with the Board was that of Assistant Director of Labor Affairs…During this period, she also received her Master's Degree from the University of Detroit and did work on an Educational Specialist Degree at Wayne State University. Advance degree work was also pursued at the University of Michigan. Louise did take a year's leave from the Board to become Congressman George Crockett's Executive Assistant in charge of his Detroit Office.

Barry Harris

Upon retiring from the Detroit Public School System, Louise was hired by the Archdiocese of Detroit and became Principal of St. Francis D'Assissi Catholic School. Upon its closing, this school became a charter school where she remained as Principal until she retired at the end of five years. During this time, Louise attended Harvard University Principal's Center and was invited to attend Oxford University's Roundtable on Charter Schools in Oxford, England. Most recently, she attended the Mexican American Cultural Center in San Antonio, Texas where she studied Spanish in an intensive setting.

Barry Harris grew up on the Near Eastside of Detroit and attended Garfield Elementary and Intermediate School and Northeastern High School in the 1940's. Exposed to piano lessons at the age of 4 by his piano playing mother, Harris became immersed in jazz in the mid 1940's. He later switched from church music to jazz music Harris started his career playing at high school dances and other social affairs. Like many Detroit musicians, Harris was nurtured by the Detroit's extraordinary school system, which cultivated an exceptional group of young and aspiring musicians that included Tommy Flanagan, Donald Byrd, Milton Jackson and

Yusef Lateef. Harris has worked with Miles Davis, Yusef Lateef, Wes Montgomery, Thelonious Monk and Coleman Hawkins. Harris returns to Detroit each year for a Kwanzaa Benefit Jazz Concert at First Unitarian Universalist Church in Detroit.

The Honorable Teola Cranon Hunter is a native Detroiter and Near Eastsider, mother, grandmother, entrepreneur, and teacher and highly

The Honorable Teola Cranon Hunter

respected political leader in Detroit, Wayne County and the State of Michigan.

She taught in the Detroit Public Schools for fourteen years, then founded Buttons and Bows Nursery and Kindergarten. In 1974, she developed an additional nursery and a preparatory school, which went to the third grade.

In 1980, Mrs. Hunter was elected to the Michigan House of Representatives where she served for eleven years. While there, she was Chairperson of the House Social Service and Youth Committee and a sub-committee Chair of the Committee on Aids. She established a non-profit foundation to help children and families affected with or by Aids, (REACT) "Resource Endowment Aiding Children Together." In 1989, she was the first female to be elected by her colleagues to the position of Speaker Pro Tempore.

In November 1992, Mrs. Hunter was the first female to be elected to the office of Wayne County Clerk. Adding another first to her accomplishments, she was the first African-American female to be appointed by a gubernatorial candidate to run for Lieutenant Governor.

Mrs. Hunter resigned from the office of Wayne County Clerk in 2000 and soon afterwards, became the founding partner of the Sloan/Hunter Group, a lobbying and consultant business specializing in Public Affairs Services and Fund Development.

In 1975, **Dr. Arthur Jefferson** became the first African-American to be appointed Detroit's Superintendent of School. Jefferson grew up on the Near Eastside of Detroit and attended Northeastern High School. Always interested in education, Jefferson never imagined that his concern s with education would eventuate in his becoming Superintendent of the Detroit Public Schools, a position he held for 13 years. Dr. Johnson had a record of high achievement as Executive Secretary of the Detroit Branch of the National Association of Colored People, which he had developed into the second largest contributing branch in the nation and as Deputy Director of the State of Michigan Civil Rights Commission

Ron Milner Playwright

Ron Milner was a Detroiter who grew up on Ferry Street on the Near Eastside and became a nationally known writer and playwright. Milner won many awards for his plays, three of which have appeared on Broadway. Among his more famous plays is "What the Wine Sellers Buy," that opened on Broadway in 1974 with a stellar cast that included Denzel Washington, Ruby Dee and Paul Winfield, "Checkmates" in 1988 with Giancaarlo Esposito and "Don't Get God Started" in 1987 with a music score written by Marvin Winans of the famous Winans family.

Milner had a stellar career as writer and director, working with such greats as Langston Hughes. Yet, Milner chose to remain in Detroit near the area in which he grew up. Milner wrote of real, struggling but proud men and women, people not too different from some of the people that he had encountered in his life. Milner's last play was "Jazz Set" produced by Plowshares in 2000. When Milner died in June 2005, he left a world enriched by his writings that revealed the heart and soul of the black struggle against the odds.

Della Reese had many "firsts." She was the first performer to perform Gospel music in Las Vegas. She was the first woman to host *The Tonight show*. Della became the first black woman to host her own nationally syndicated television talk show.

In 1983, following a near fatal aneurysm, Della was inspired by her seemingly miraculous recovery to become a minister. As an ordained minister of the Church "Understanding Principals for a Better Living" in Los Angeles, Della preaches every Sunday to a standing room only crowd. In 1997, G.P. Putnam's Sons published Her autobiography, "Angels Along the Way" that acknowledges the help of the human "angels' who stepped into her life, giving guidance and support.

Reginald Wilson Ph.D., a Near Eastsider, is perhaps best known in Detroit's educational circles as President of Wayne County Community College, a position he held for ten years. Other positions he has held in higher education have been dean, director of test development and research, director of black studies, and director of Upward Bound. Dr. Wilson has taught graduate courses in psychology, black studies and Educational and Public Policy at Wayne State University, the University of Detroit, Oakland University and the

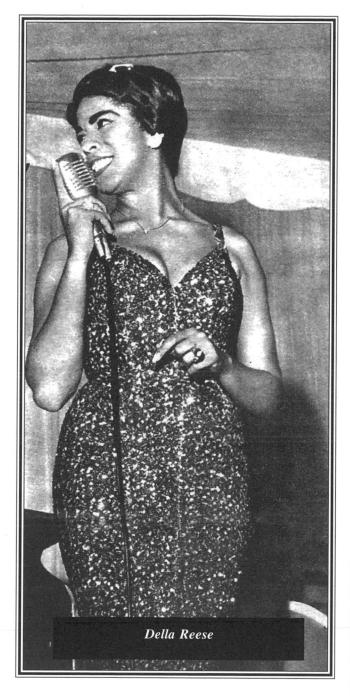

Della Reese

Reginald Wilson, Ph.D.

Della Reese was born Delores Early and grew up on the Near Eastside of Detroit. She attended and graduated from Northeastern High School in 1949. Della began singing as a 6 year old in the church her parents attended. As a 13 year old, she went on her first professional tour, singing backup for Mahalia Jackson. By 1953 Della Reese had a recording contract and two hit singles, "In the Still of the Night" and "Don't you Know." In that same year, Della Reese formed her own group, the Meditation singers.

University of Michigan. He was also a visiting professor at the University of Texas L.B. Johnson School of Public Policy.

In October 1988 Dr. Wilson was appointed Senior Scholar Emeritus of the American Council on Education. He originally joined the Council in 1981, as the Director of the Office of Minority Conceerns.He is an Honorary Degree recipient from the City University of New York, LaGuardia Community College, the State University of New York, Plattsburgh, and St. John's University.

Dr. Wilson received his Ph.D. in clinical and educational psychology from Wayne State University and is a licensed Psychologist in Michigan and Washington, D.C. He was honored as a Distinguished Alumnus of Wayne State University and is a recipient of the Anthony Wayne Award, and the Distinguished Service Medal of the City of Detroit. He has also received the Harold Delaney Exemplary Leadership Award from the American Association of Higher Education.

Dr. Wilson has authored numerous books, articles, and research studies during his career in higher education. He is on the editorial board of the American Board of Education, The Urban Review, About Campus, and New Politics. He is author of *Civil Liberties and the U.S.*, and a co-author of *Human Development in the Urban Community*.

Dr. Wilson is a founding member of the Jim Dandy Ski Club, an organization that has expanded nationwide. Dr. Wilson is also a founding member of the Black Psychologists, a national professional organization.

Willie Horton, who in 1963 became the first black baseball player for the Detroit Tigers, grew up in the Brewster Projects on Detroit's Near Eastside as the youngest of nineteen children. As a boy, Willie reports sneaking into the Tiger stadium to watch his heroes play baseball. As a sandlot star in Detroit, Willie drew attention at the age of 16 when he blasted a homerun into Tiger Stadium's right field stands in an All-City game. He was a powerfully built man. It is said that it once took four teammates to keep the slugger from beating an opposing pitcher after a brush back pitch

Willie Horton

Horton's career as a player for the Detroit Tigers was a stellar one. His statistics are awesome. In his first two full seasons with the Detroit Tigers, Willie hit a total of 56 home runs and drove in a total of 204 runs. During the 1965 season, in seven games at Washington and Boston, Willie hit six home runs, five doubles and batted in 16 runs. He was voted starting outfielder for the All-Star game. Willie hit two homeruns in a game 30 times during his career. In the 1968 World Series, Willie earned a batting average of .304. He scored six runs, hit one homerun and had three RBI propelling the Tigers to a World Series seven games win over the St. Louis Cardinals.

Today, Willie Horton has a foundation in his name that is dedicated to helping disadvantaged youngsters who grew up in circumstances similar to his own. A 160-page book has been written honoring Horton's contributions to Detroit. The book, "Willie Horton, Detroit's Own Willie the Wonder," by authors Grant Eldridge and Karen Elizabeth Bush is one in the Detroit Biography Series for Young Readers. Willie is a member of

Gilbert Alan Maddox

Detroit's Black community. The series production served as a TV workshop for area writers, musicians, graphic artists and production assistants. This series launched the career of Tony Brown and "Black Journal," "Detroit's Black Journal" and "Profiles in Black."

Among his many achievements, Dr. Maddox hosted "Profiles in Blacks," a prime-time series broadcast by WWJ-TV and later by WDIV-TV, In More than 600 programs. The historic series featured on-location interviews with a variety of Detroiters, including Marvin Gaye, Smoky Robinson, Rosa Parks and basketball's Bill Russell. From 1983 to 1985, Dr. Maddox co-hosted Detroit's first news magazine series with one of his former students, Carmen Harlan, on WDIV-TV.

Dr. Maddox has held a variety of administrative and teaching positions at several universities, including Howard University, University of Michigan, Wayne State University, and Michigan State University. He has won a number of honors, Mayor's Distinguished Service Award, City of Detroit, Merit Award, Detroit's Common

the Detroit Tigers Organization and represents the organization at civic and business functions. A statue of Willie Horton reposes at Comerica Park

Gilbert Alan Maddox was born in Detroit at the height of the Great Depression After his father's untimely death, Gilbert grew up with his mother and brother in the Brewster Projects. He attended Lincoln, Bishop and Sacred Heart School, all on Detroit's Near Eastside. He became an educator and taught at Stephen Foster, Northeastern and Jefferson Jr. High. Additionally, Maddox was a swimming instructor at Brewster Center, Peck, Miller Jr. High and at Balch Elementary. Among Maddox's credentials are a B.A. in Business Administration, Elementary and Secondary School teaching certificates, a Master's degree in Speech, and a Doctorate degree in Radio-Television-Film, all from Wayne State University, the first African-American to earn this coveted honor.

A pioneer in the broadcast field Maddox hosted and produced "Black and Unknown Bands," an eighteen program series dramatizing the writing of such black authors and writers as Langston Hughes. He later produced a series entitled CPT that featured the news, history and culture of

Dr. Barbara Ross-Lee

Council Distinguished Alumni Award, Wayne State University and Top Public Affairs Series from Variety Magazine, 1971-1973, given to "Profiles in Black."

Barbara Ross-Lee, D.O., older sister of Diana Ross, was born in Detroit and grew up in the inner city. Although Ross-Lee shared Diana's love for music, she made her mark in the sciences. Ross-Lee graduated from Wayne State University in 1965 with a B.S. in biology and chemistry then taught in the Detroit Public Schools. In 1969, she entered Michigan State University of Osteopathic Medicine in Pontiac. After graduating in 1973, she ran a family practice. In 1984, Ross-Lee joined the U.S. Department of Health and Human Services as a consultant on education in the health professions. She became community representative on the

Dr. Robert L. Ellison

Michigan Governor's Minority Health Advisory from 1990 to 1993. .

In 1993, Ross-Lee became the first African-American woman dean of a United States medical school at the College of Osteopathic Medicine of Ohio University until 2001. In 2001, Dr. Ross-Lee was appointed vice president for Health Sciences and Medical Affairs at the New York Institute of Technology. In 2002, she became dean of the New York Institute of Technology's College of Osteopathic Medicine. Dr. Ross-Lee is a Fellow of the American Osteopathic Boards of Family Physicians.

Mary Wilson

Mary Wilson is a former and founding member of the Supremes. She was born in Mississippi and grew up in the Brewster Projects in an apartment she described as making her feel as elated as if she was living in a high rise on Park Avenue. Mary attended Bishop School and Northeastern High School in Detroit. Mary's original group, called the Primettes and included Diana Ross, Florence Ballard and Betty McGlown started on a path to fame by competing in the Detroit /Windsor International Freedom Festival amateur talent contest in and *winning*. This was the first time that the Primettes had received money for a performance, a total of $15.00. This win accelerated the group's drive to become rich and famous. Mary's history as a member of the Supremes was the inspiration for her autobiography, "Dreamgirl," published by St. Martin's Press in 1986.

John L. Kline, Ph.D.

Robert L. Ellison, **D.D.S**. a Near Eastsider, attended Balch Elementary School, Garfield Intermediate School and Northeastern High School. Always an honor student, Ellison was also an outstanding athlete. He attended Wayne State University and earned his B.S. Degree in Pharmacy from the College of Pharmacy. While attending Wayne State, he was a starting guard on the nationally ranked varsity basketball team for three seasons.

Upon graduation from Wayne State University, Dr. Ellison attended Meharry Medical College School of Dentistry earning his D.D.S. in 1960. He received advanced specialty education in Endonocs at the University of Pennsylvia Graduate School in Medicine and advanced specialty education in Oral Pathology at the Oral Pathology School of Dental Medicine. Ellison received an M.S. Degree from the School of Pharmacology at Temple. Ellison became the first African American certified Endodontist in the United States.

After Dr. Ellison's return to Detroit, he became a full professor in the Department of Endodontics at the University of Michigan. He was a member of the graduate Endodontics Faculty at the University of Detroit School of Dentistry. Ellison

served also as adjunct professor at Case Western School of Dentistry in Cleveland Ohio, the Meharry School of Dentistry and Howard University School of Dentistry. Dr. Ellison was a Diplomate of the American Board of Endodontics and a past president of the Wolverine Dental Society. As a Captain in the U.S. Air Force at Castle Air Force Base in Merced California, Ellison served as the Base Endodontist.

John L. Kline, Ph.D., a Near Eastsider, is an All-American basketball player from Wayne University in Detroit, Michigan. He joined the Harlem Globetrotters in 1953 and traveled the world playing for them until 1959. His eyes were open to many lifestyles in China, Japan, Indonesia, Singapore, the Philippines, Australia, New Zealand, Central and South America, Cuba and the African continent. John was a celebrity and as a player for the "Trotters," he met and dined with many of the dignitaries of those countries. When he returned to Detroit in 1960, devoid of his celebrity status, John retreated into the hellhole of drugs and to alcohol addiction. Not one to be defeated, John had the perseverance and the will power to pick himself up and return to Wayne University where he earned his Bachelors, his Masters and a Ph.D. in the history and philosophy of education.

91

John started his own company on health promotion and wellness and was appointed by Mayor Coleman A. Young as the Director of Drug Prevention Services, a position held for seven years. He became the Director of Drug Free Schools and Communities for the Detroit Public Schools. Governor Blanchard, recognizing Kline's expertise in substance abuse, appointed him to the Michigan Board of Nursing at a time when internal substance abuse was a problem.

Kline founded and is president of Black Legends of Professional Basketball Foundation, which has done much to recognize and to support the many pioneer players who paved the way for the National Basketball Association. In 1986, Kline developed the Youth Athletic Enrichment ((YAEP) Program in Detroit's middle schools. This program is designed to plant the seeds of a better lifestyle and to open the eyes of all students through the leader/athlete concept in Inner City Middle Schools. Dr. Kline's vision is to take this program national by launching it in the 27 Inner- Cities where NBA teams play their home games.

Dr. Kline has been inducted into the African-American Hall of Fame, the Wayne State University Hall of Fame, the Michigan Sports Hall of Fame and the Harlem Globetrotters exclusive Legends Circle. John is the author of seven published books.

Leonard Ellison, M.D. was born and lived on Farnsworth on Detroit's Near Eastside. He attended Balch Elementary and Garfield Intermediate schools and Northern High School. After dropping out of high school, Ellison spent two years serving his Country. He used the G.I. Bill he had earned and enrolled in the pharmacy program at the Institute of Technology. He then transferred to Wayne State University School of Pharmacy where he and his brother, Robert comprised one-half of the black student population in that discipline.

Following the granting of his degree in Pharmacy, Leonard entered Medical school at the University of Michigan. After completing medical school, Ellison completed General Internship at Hurley Hospital in Flint. He then entered training

Alma Grace Russell Stallworth

in his specialty, Psychiatry, at Northville State Hospital.

The Honorable Alma Grace Russell Stallworth served in the Michigan House of Representatives for twenty-five years. As a legislator, Stallworth was an innovator, chairing the Michigan Legislative Black Caucus and founding the Black Caucus Foundation of Michigan. The Foundation is celebrating its 22nd year as a non-profit, community- based organization that sponsors many programs that help middle and high school students develop life skills and make healthy decisions. These programs enroll over a thousand students annually and generate several thousand pledges by students to lead a drug and violence free life.

Dr. Stallworth has studied legislatives systems abroad as a member of *Women in Government* visiting the Orient, Germany, Italy, Japan, England and South Africa. She has received a Master's Degree in Health Education and Promotion and a Doctorate in Government Administration from Chelsea University of London, England.

Inducted into the Alpha Kappa Alpha Sorority as an honorary member, Stallworth sponsored Super Anchor Parties for UNCF for ten

Murray Jackson, Poet & Educator

Diana Ross

years. Those parties have generated over a million dollars.

Murray Jackson was a poet, educator and longtime political and civic activist. In his younger years, Jackson lived with his family on Garfield Street between Brush and John R. A Near Eastside resident, Jackson attended Trowbridge Elementary and Garfield Intermediate School.

After serving in World War 11, Jackson entered Wayne State University where he earned a bachelor's and master's degree in Humanities. Jackson subsequently became assistant dean of students and assistant to the vice president for urban affairs. He was a professor at the University of Michigan Center for the Study of Higher Education and was the founding President of Wayne County Community College. In December 2001, Jackson was awarded the Doctor of Humane Letters degree, an honorary doctorate from Wayne State University

Jackson was the first executive director for the Detroit Council of the Arts and a Chairman of the First District of the Democratic Party from 1964-1969. In 1964, Jackson and his first wife, Dauris became the first African-Americans since Reconstruction to be seated at the Michigan Democratic Convention.

In December 2001, The WSU Board of Governors recognized Jackson's many years of service with an endowed scholarship in his name and appointed him Governor Emeritus.

As a poet, Jackson both wrote and taught poetry. He wrote poetry collections, *Woodland Sketches*: *Scenes From Childhood* (1990) and *Watermelon Rinds and Cherry Pits* (1991). He contributed poetry to a number of publications and anthologies.

Jackson died in 2002. There are many other Near Eastsiders, equally impressive, but too numerous to elaborate on. Many you may know. Among them are:

Diana Ross who grew up in the Brewster Housing Projects is best known perhaps as a member of the original Supremes, but she is also known as a talented actress, Diva and the lead singer of the original Supremes. She has made her mark in motion pictures, music and the theatre. She starred in three feature movies that exhibited some of her versatility as an artist. They are *Lady Sings the Blues* in which she portrays Billie Holiday,

Charles N. Boyce

Hugh Lawson

Mahogany *with* Billy Dee Williams and Anthony Perkins; also *The Wiz,* portraying Dorothy in a black version of *The Wizard of Oz.* Ms. Ross is said to have made provisions for scholarships for Florence Ballard's three children.

Florence Ballard was one of the original *Primettes* later renamed *The Supremes.* Like Diana, Florence was raised in the Brewster Housing Projects. Her voice was magnificent and voluminous. Florence did well as a member of the Supremes until Diana Ross was named lead singer. This diminution of her role as an equal in the Supremes may have started Florence on her downward spiral. After Ms. Ballard left the Supremes, she never regained primacy as a singer. She died at the age of 32.

Charles N. Boyce, entrepreneur, one of five Boyce Brothers, has had a varied career. Although he was a star athlete at Northwestern High School, his professional path has been primarily in business. An active philanthropist, businessman and civic leader, Boyce is a member of the Detroit Urban League, the NAACP, the Booker T. Washington Business Association, the Southern Christian Leadership Conference and many other professional and civic groups. Boyce has been a member of the Detroit Housing Commission, Urban Alliance and the Michigan Inkster Association of Black Business and Engineering Students. Boyce's interests have been far ranging. They have led him into such diverse activities as casino development and the development of affordable housing for Detroit's residents. Boyce is the founder and leader of The James Boyce Foundation that honors his younger brother, James Boyce who died in 2001.

———————

Hugh J. Lawson was born on Rowena Street, now Mack, in March 1935. He lived in the Brewster Projects until age sixteen. . He attended Lincoln Elementary, Garfield Intermediate and Cass Technical High School. Born into a musically inclined family, his music training began with piano lessons at the age of three. His musical training was continued at Garfield Intermediate where he was a member of the Garfield orchestra and was enhanced at Cass Tech. He studied clarinet and tenor saxophone as well as piano. Hugh attended

Wayne State University where he studied music composition.

Lawson's professional career began in 1956 when he joined the Yusef Lateef Quintet, playing at the Klein's Show Bar on Twelfth Street. In 1960, Hugh left Detroit for New York with the Yusef Lateef Quintet with whom he recorded for more than ten years.

In subsequent years, Hugh performed and recorded with a virtual encyclopedia of Jazz Artists, including Sonny Rollins, Harry "Sweets" Edison, Kenny Burrell, Stanley Turrentine, Wes Montgomery, Roy Eldridge, Charlie Mingus and Eddie "Lockjaw' Davis. Hugh did stints and recorded with Gloria Lynn, Joe Williams and Dinah Washington.

Hugh's credits include three featured recordings: *Prime Time* on the Storyville label, *Colour* on Soul Note Records and *Casablanca* on Something Else Records. He was also one of the founders of the "Piano Choir."

One of Hugh's proudest moments was being named as one of the Five World Class Pianists in an article, "Motor City Classicists" that appeared in the Village Voice in 1983, written by Gary Giddens. The Five listed were Hank Jones. Tommy Flanagan, Barry Harris, Roland Hanna and Hugh Lawson. Hugh passed away at age 61 on March 11, 1997. He was married to his childhood sweetheart, Florence Rowlette Lawson, a Near Eastsider.

———————

Bernard Johnson, a professor of dance and costume design at the University of California at Irvine and professor of art at the Fashion Institute of Design in New York City, wore many hats. Among them, dancer, choreographer, and fashion and costume designer. It is said that he wore them all with the aplomb of a king. Born and

raised on the Near Eastside by his parents, John Henry Johnson Sr. and his mother May Lizzie Cooper Johnson, Johnson graduated with honors from Cass Technical High School in 1954 and accepted a scholarship offer from the New York City Fashion Institute of Design. Johnson received a Bachelor of Arts degree in 1957.

Johnson studied ballet, modern, tap and jazz dance in Detroit where he began his professional career training with distinguished teachers, Honi Coles and Hamya Holm as well as LeClaire Knox

Bernard Johnson

and Mary Ann Clemons. As a youngster, Johnson appeared on many cultural and classical events in Detroit. While still a teen-ager, Bernard Johnson performed in New York City with Ward Fleming's New York Negro Ballet and designed costumes for the company. He also appeared with Aubrey

Hitching's Negro Dance Theater in 1956. Johnson danced in musicals on and OFF Broadway including the Broadway production of "On a Clear Day You Can See Forever" and City Center productions of "Fiorello" and "Showboat." He also performed with Cleo Quitman, his former wife, as a cabaret act that toured Europe and was featured at the Apollo and in the Catskills during the 1960's. He danced in the 1980 Off Broadway review "Stompin' at the Savoy," and directed the Off Broadway musical "Back in the Big Time" in 1986.

Johnson choreographed the Broadway and national tour production of "Ain't Supposed to Die a Natural Death," the 1975 film "The Bingo Long Traveling All-Stars and Motor Kings," and acts for Melba Moore, the Manhattans and shows at the Apollo, Madison Square Garden, the Sands Hotel and Casino in Las Vegas and Café Versailles in New York. His choreographic credits also include two command performances for King Hassan II in Morocco in the early 1990's.

Johnson, euphemistically called "the Hope Diamond" of fashion design, created stylish, witty and vividly colored costumes. His Broadway design credits include "Waltz of the Stork," "Eubie," "Guys a and Dolls," "Bubbling Brown Sugar" and "Raisin." Mr. Johnson deigned costumes for the New York City Ballet, Dance Theater of Harlem, the Joffrey Ballet, Ballet Hispanico, and for many rock and jazz musicians.

His film credits include the 1990 "New Jack City. " His television credits include costumes for "The Merv Griffin Show," and specials for Bill Cosby, Harry Belafonte and Lena Horne. He has created wardrobes for Gregory Hines, Savion Glover, the Isley Brothers and for shows by Judy Garland and Josephine Baker.

Mr. Johnson was a member of The Black Filmmakers Hall of Fame. He taught jazz dance in Moscow in1992 under the auspices of the American Dance Festival.

———

Council Cargle, Ruby Dee and Ron Milner audio-taping Ron Milner's play "Checkmates."

CHAPTER SIX
Black Owned Businesses a Tradition

Turning Discrimination into Economic Opportunities

The tradition of black owned businesses in Detroit is legendary. Long before the great migration of southern black Americans to Detroit in the early twentieth century, a favorable climate for business had existed. The 1910 census reported that Detroit's Negro population was 5,741 and that 25 places of business were black owned. By 1920, the black population was 40,000 and African-Americans owned 360 businesses in Detroit. Among them was a movie theater, the only black owned pawnshop in the United States, a co-op grocery and a bank. The black community is reported to have also had 17 physicians, 22 lawyers, 22 barber shops, 13 dentists, 12 cartage agencies, 11 tailors, 10 restaurants, 10 real estate dealers, eight grocers, six drug stores, five undertakers, four employment offices, a few garages and a candy maker. By 1930, the black population of Detroit had skyrocketed to 120,000.

From the 1920's through the 1950's, the growth of a large and relatively prosperous black population fueled the proliferation of black businesses. When Henry Ford began the recruitment of black people to work in the automobile industry, there was a great migration of blacks from the rural south. Many of these people had incomes sufficient to support the many businesses that populated the Near Eastside. Their incomes afforded them the opportunity to buy and to do things that they were denied in the bigotry of the South. For the many who had been burdened by low wages and racial injustices, this Paradise Valley on the Near Eastside was truly a "land of milk and honey."

Hundreds of black-owned businesses emerged to serve the southern blacks that had migrated to Detroit following World War 1. The concentration of so many people on the near eastside meant great opportunities for businessmen and professionals. Black entrepreneurs built a wide range of businesses, drugstores, beauty parlors, medical practices, restaurants and nightclubs. These institutions were able to provide almost anything a person needed. The segregationist practices of white owned and operated businesses that existed in Detroit contributed to the growth of black businesses by giving black owned businesses a captive market. Despite the fact that local banks would not make loans to black entrepreneurs, their businesses flourished. Detroit gained a national reputation as a haven for black business.

During the high point of black owned businesses, black entrepreneurs had to really struggle to make their businesses work. No city contracts existed to assist the black business community. No wealthy backers waited in the wings to provide capital to build or expand black owned businesses or to bail out a business in trouble. Mentors or those with expertise in business were few. What many entrepreneurs did have was the vision, the belief that they could make a comfortable living providing the goods and services the black community needed and they had the courage to pursue that vision. Today, many of the prominent businesses of the 30's and 40's are gone. Some few of them live on and hopefully may provide impetus and inspiration for newer generations of entrepreneurs...

Bertha Hansbury School of Music and Household Art Guild

Bertha Hansbury was a talented musician who is said to have had dreams of becoming a concert pianist. Hansbury had received classical music training at the Detroit Conservatory of Music and also in Germany. She gave up her dream of becoming a concert pianist in favor of establishing a music school for black children.

Bertha Hansbury and her Husband, Williams H. Phillips purchased a red brick Victorian home at 544 E. Frederick built in the early 1890's by James Owen, one of the developers of Indian Village. In 1925, the Bertha Hansbury Music School was opened in their home. It was the first music school in Detroit to bring black children and teachers together in a classroom. Along with many music courses, there were classes in etiquette, history and interpretive dance. This school nurtured thousands of young African-Americans in music. The Hansbury Music School also housed a state licensed and accredited kindergarten and nursery school. The Household Art Guild, an agency licensed by the state, served as the first employment agency for African-Americans in Detroit. It pre-dated the first government supported job agency by more than ten years. Though Hansbury taught and tutored many of Detroit's black children, the school did not survive the Great Depression.

Barthwell's Drugstores

Sidney Barthwell received his pharmacy degree from Detroit City College in 1931. Although he was a pharmacist, Mr. Barthwell was most famous for the ice cream parlors that dotted the landscape along Hastings Street corridor in the 1930s-1950s. Mr. Barthwell was what is euphemistically called, " a man with a plan." He had a vision that he could serve the primarily African American community by providing a

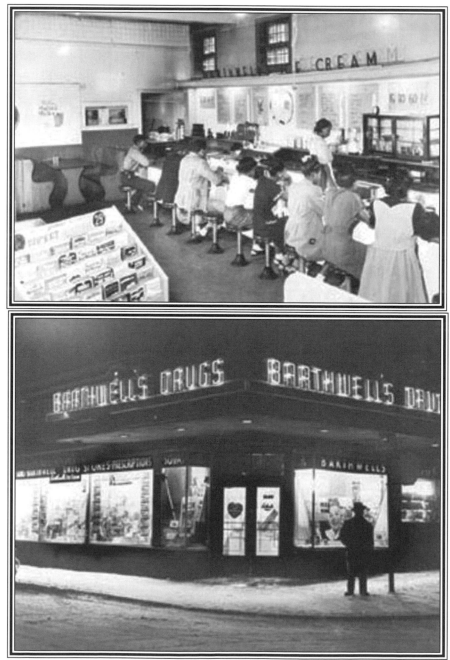

product that most people love, namely ice cream. Barthwell is said to have borrowed venture capital ($500) and parlayed that money into his first drugstore. It wasn't long before Barthwell had a chain of drugstores/soda fountains throughout Detroit serving a brand of ice cream that he himself created Barthwell's Drug Stores, Inc., was the largest chain of black owned drugstores in the U.S.A. Mr. Barthwell gave many African-American youths their first job and employed hundreds of African-Americans in the city.

Many Detroiters remember with great fondness, Barthwell's ice cream. These Barthwell fans recall the many wonderful flavors that were available to them. They remember too, the generous size of the ice cream servings that could be purchased for a nickel or a dime. Looking back, it seems that no one man was more responsible for the happiness that so many Detroiters derived from eating a double dip ice cream cone on a hot summer day or night than was Mr. Barthwell.

THE EAGLE MOVING COMPANY

In 1920, at the age of 25, Alfred Greenfield started the Eagle Moving Company It was a home based business located at 602 East Warren on the corner of Warren and St. Antoine. Mr. Greenfield started his business with 2 small trucks and did mostly local moving. As his company grew, he was able to purchase eight vans, four (4) large and four (4) small. With the acquisition of these new vans, Greenfield was able to do long distance and local moving for businesses as well as for individual customers.

The Eagle Moving Company was the first black owned moving company that did local and long distance moving. The company maintained contracts with the Sears Roebuck Company and the old Federal Department Store chain to deliver household appliances.

When the business site on Warren and Rivard was demolished to make way for the expressway, the Eagle Moving Company was relocated to Fenkell and Livernois. Greenfield continued to run a successful business at this location until his retirement in 1968.

Sidney Barthwell

Alfred & Naomi Greenfield, Owners of Eagle Moving Company.

Diggs Funeral Homes or The House of Diggs

Charles C. Diggs founded the Diggs family funeral home in 1921. Located at 689-693 Mack Avenue, it quickly became the largest and allegedly the finest black-owned funeral home in Michigan. For many years no family name was better known or more highly regarded than the Diggs family name. Charles C. Diggs, Sr. was the acknowledged founder of the Detroit Memorial Cemetery Association in association with Dr. Aaron Toodle, a pharmacist. The cemetery itself is where most black people were and continue to be buried. Charles C. Diggs, Sr. was the first black man elected to the Michigan State Senate.

His son, Charles C. Diggs, Jr. became the first black person from Michigan to be elected to the United States House of Representatives. Both of their political lives were touched by scandal during their times in office.

Ed Brazelton, Florist

This extraordinary man, Ed Brazelton, at age 91 was still fairly active in the business that he started in 1941 until his death in 2006. Brazleton came to Detroit in 1935 by way of Cleveland from Birmingham, Alabama. The son of a bootlegger,

he began in the business selling flowers on the street for 25 cents a bundle. The first flowers Brazleton sold were paper flowers because he could not purchase cut or live flowers from the wholesale vendors. . Two years later, Brazleton opened his first shop, Acme Flowers on Brush Street and Alexandrine. At that time, Brazleton lived on Willis and Brush streets. Later, he moved his business to 12th Street, and finally to West Grand Boulevard. Today, there are 10 employees at Brazleton's Florist with Brazleton's son, Ed Brazleton 111 as owner/manager. This still flourishing business sells not only plants and flowers, but also, balloons and stuffed animals. Most of the businesses of the 30's 40' and 50's are gone, but Brazelton's Florist still thrives as a memorial to the man who devoted much of his life to the development of organizations that benefited the black community.

Brazleton was a civic and social activist. He helped start or was at the helm of many organizations, including the First Independence

Harold Kutner, GM's Vice President of Purchasing presents the Michigan Minority Business Development Council Award to Edgar Brazelton

Edgar Brazelton (seated right) with Foursome Golf Club Winners.

National Bank, Home Federal Savings and Loan, the Booker T. Washington Trade Association and the Paradise Valley Business Association. Brazelton was one of the early members of the Cotillion Club. This social club used its political muscle to integrate Detroit's police department and other institutions.

Ed Davis... Studebaker Dealer

Ed Davis was distinguished twice over. When Ed Davis opened Davis Motor Sales in 1939, a used car dealership, he became the first African in America to do so. In 1940, Studebaker Motor Car Company of South Bend Indiana awarded Ed Davis a franchise to sell new Studebakers. Again, Davis was a first. He became the first African-American new car dealer in the United States. Davis located his business on the Near East Side in the heart of the black community. Davis was rewarded for his faith in the black community; he soon became a leading new car dealer in the Detroit

area. Davis ran his business successfully until 1956, shortly before Studebaker Motor Car Company went out of business.

The Blue Goose Restaurant

In 1927, Abdul Muthleb opened a restaurant called "The Blue Goose." This restaurant was located at 583 Alexanderine at St. Antoine. In 1933, the Blue Goose was relocated to 4121 Hastings Street. Mr. Muthleb managed this restaurant at this location for over 25 years.

On Monday through Friday, the restaurant catered to factory workers and laborers. On Sundays, the factory workers and laborers would bring their families to the restaurant after church

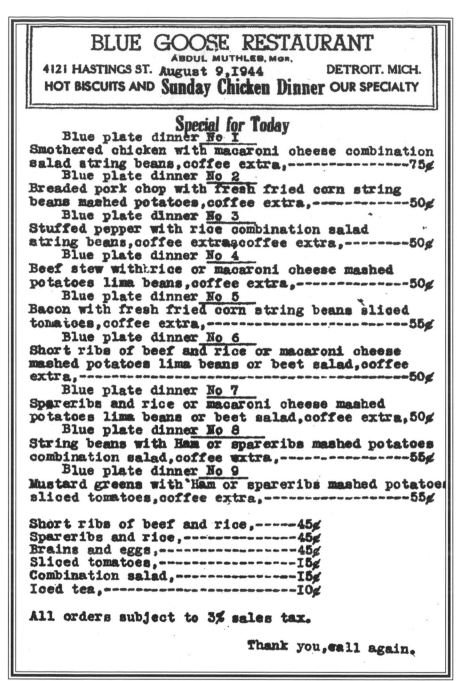

BLUE GOOSE RESTAURANT

ABDUL MUTHLEB, MGR.

4121 HASTINGS ST. August 9, 1944 DETROIT. MICH.

HOT BISCUITS AND **Sunday Chicken Dinner** OUR SPECIALTY

Special for Today

Blue plate dinner No 1
Smothered chicken with macaroni cheese combination
salad string beans,coffee extra,----------------75¢
    Blue plate dinner No 2
Breaded pork chop with fresh fried corn string
beans mashed potatoes,coffee extra,------------50¢
    Blue plate dinner No 3
Stuffed pepper with rice combination salad
string beans,coffee extra,coffee extra,--------50¢
    Blue plate dinner No 4
Beef stew with rice or macaroni cheese mashed
potatoes lima beans,coffee extra,--------------50¢
    Blue plate dinner No 5
Bacon with fresh fried corn string beans sliced
tomatoes,coffee extra,-------------------------55¢
    Blue plate dinner No 6
Short ribs of beef and rice or macaroni cheese
mashed potatoes lima beans or beet salad,coffee
extra,---50¢
    Blue plate dinner No 7
Spareribs and rice or macaroni cheese mashed
potatoes lima beans or beet salad,coffee extra,50¢
    Blue plate dinner No 8
String beans with Ham or spareribs mashed potatoes
combination salad,coffee extra,----------------55¢
    Blue plate dinner No 9
Mustard greens with Ham or spareribs mashed potatoes
sliced tomatoes,coffee extra,------------------55¢

Short ribs of beef and rice,------45¢
Spareribs and rice,---------------45¢
Brains and eggs,------------------45¢
Sliced tomatoes,------------------15¢
Combination salad,----------------15¢
Iced tea,-------------------------10¢

All orders subject to 3% sales tax.

        Thank you, call again.

The restaurant owner extended credit to many of its customers. More often than not, the workers would spend most of their earnings over the weekend. Mr. Muthleb made liberal use of a "meal ticket" system. On Friday (payday) the customer would purchase a ticket from the restaurant for a set price. This card, prepaid, would enable the customer to eat a meal and pay for it by presenting the card. The card was purchased to indicate that it was used to pay for a meal. This convenience was very popular with the customers.

The daily menu met the needs of the customer by presenting several " blue plate" special dinners. See the copy of an original menu dated August 9, 1944.

THE BOOKER T. WASHINGTON TRADE ASSOCIATION

services for dinner. The Sunday special was usually a fried chicken dinner with hot biscuits.

The pastry chef was responsible for the fried apple and sweet potato pies and biscuits. The restaurant enjoyed the reputation of having the best pies and biscuits of all the restaurants in the area. If a customer could not find a particular cut of meat (steak or chops) on the menu, Mr. Muthleb would send for it at the grocery store and prepare it for the customer. This personals service positively enhanced the reputation of the Blue Goose restaurant.

The Booker T. Washington Trade Association was one of the many black businesses housed in the Detroit Memorial Building on 446 East Warren. The association was founded in 1930 by a small group of black professionals headed by activist minister, the Reverend William Peck of Bethel A.M.E. church. Reverend Peck saw the need to help the many southern blacks that had come to

Detroit fleeing the double-edged sword of racism and poverty.

1930 was a time of economic crisis for America. For African-Americans, especially the job seekers who had migrated from the south, the need was even greater. Black businesses were denied loan services from the banks. One solution was to assist in the development of self-help efforts and to retain and expand businesses owned and run by African-Americans. The success of the mission may be evaluated by some of the achievements of members who made it big in Detroit and in Michigan. One of the notables is Richard Austin, former Secretary of State for the State of Michigan. Another success story is Mel Farr who at one time was the largest African-American new car dealer in the United States.

Dr. Violet Harrison Lewis
Founder, Detroit College of Business.

Lewis College of Business

1940 Census records showed that of 12,000 black women at work in Detroit, about 80% worked as domestics or in personal service. Some few worked as mail handlers or in the school system. Many of these women were the sole support or the main support of their families. Most were undereducated and lacked the skills that would allow them to prosper in a labor market where racial segregation and discrimination were normal practices.

In the late 30's and early 40's, secretarial training programs and other vocational schools in Detroit excluded black students. In 1938, Dr. Violet Lewis moved to Detroit after being invited by the Detroit Chamber of Commerce to open a business school that would train black women for careers in business. This she did, buying a large Neo-Colonial style home on Ferry Street and John R.

Not everyone was pleased that a black woman had bought an elegant home in the Merrill Palmer neighborhood. Six months after moving there, Dr. Lewis was ordered to move for violating the existing zoning laws that did not allow commercial establishments. To circumvent this ruling, Dr. Lewis, with the advice and assistance of Horace White, the pastor of Plymouth Congregational Church and his attorneys, changed the designation of Lewis Business College from a for profit business to that of a non-profit.

The training offered by the Lewis College of Business filled a void that had prevented many black women from pursuing secretarial careers. The timing for opening this school could not have been better. World War II happened and there was an increased demand for trained office workers. The college flourished. Demand for training was so great that enrollment tripled and classes had to be offered in three shifts.

In 1976, Lewis College of Business had expanded its programs so much that the Ferry Street building could no longer handle the capacity. It sought larger quarters and is now located at Meyers and McNichols in Northwest Detroit. The original home of the Lewis College of Business was listed in the Michigan Registry of Historic Sites on June 30, 1988. A Michigan Historical Marker was erected on August 29, 1988 at the intersection of John R. and East Ferry.

THE GOTHAM HOTEL

The Gotham Hotel was the crown jewel of Detroit's black owned businesses. The Gotham was a nine-story building located at John R. Street and Orchestra Place and it was *Grand*. Two entrepreneurs, John White and Irving Roane, bought the Gotham in 1943. It became an immediate star and the hub of a myriad of activities, both legal and illegal. The Gotham quickly became the place to be. To the Detroiters and for the celebrities, politicians, sports stars and show people, nothing was finer than a visit to the Gotham to have dinner, to party elegantly in the Holiday Room or to spend one or some nights. The Gotham hosted such celebrities as Nat King Cole, Ella, Sarah, Billy Eckstein and Duke Ellington. This was where all of the really big people of color stayed when visiting Detroit. The Gotham was in a pivotal location, close to the entertainment district where most musicians performed and where 'the happenings' were. The Gotham was a *destination* for travelers and locals alike. The amenities were so grand, the atmosphere so special that poet Langston Hughes, in an article printed in the Chicago Defender, praised the Gotham Hotel to the skies, describing it as 'wondrous' and a minor miracle for which he thanked God.

THE RACIAL DIGEST

In January 1942, the first issue of the Racial Digest was published. Racial Digest was a periodical that focused on issues of interests to people of color. It was a monthly publication that

Lewis Business College (former James F. Murphy home), 5450 John R. & East Ferry Streets.

GOTHAM HOTEL, John R. St. and Orchestra Place, Detroit, Mich.

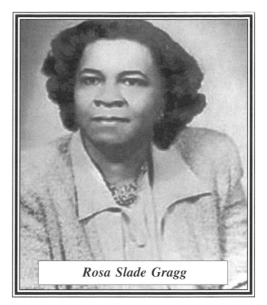

Rosa Slade Gragg

The Slade-Gragg Academy of Practical Arts

Rosa Slade Gragg was known as a social and political activist, who had served as president of the Detroit Association of Colored Women's Clubs before she founded and operated the Slade- Gragg Academy of Practical Arts. In1941, Mrs. Gragg and her husband bought the Georgian revival house on the southwest corner of Ferry and Brush because Mrs. Gragg is said to have believed that the association should have a central location and a classy address. She and her husband encountered and surmounted zoning problems designed to keep black people from owning property on that part of Ferry Street.

Between 1946 and 1952, Mrs. Gragg operated the Slade-Gragg Academy of Practical Arts. The academy offered classes in tailoring, upholstering, dressmaking and food services. Many of the students were veterans of World War 11 as well as those who served in Korea. The academy was housed in what has been described as a three-unit Arts and Crafts style building The official address was 5461 Brush Street, although technically, the location was at 326 East Ferry.

was sold by subscription for $1.00 a year or ten cents a copy. Subscriptions were received from as far away as the Canal Zone and Havana, Cuba. The Community Publishing Company, located at 3750 Russell Street in Detroit, published the Magazine. The editor was H.L. Richey. The magazine's stated aim was to present leading articles on the Negro each month from the many magazines and periodicals that existed so that Negroes would have more knowledge of events, as well as a more comprehensive picture of what America thinks about the Negro and his problems. The Racial Digest sought articles by foreign writers as well as from those born in the U.S.A. The first edition of Racial Digest reprinted articles from 12 publications including News Week Magazine, Crisis Magazine, The Nation and The Public Opinion Quarterly.

The Dunbar Hospital

During the early part of the 20th century, black physicians and black patients were barred from many of the white owned hospitals in Detroit. In 1918, a black group known as the Allied Medical Society decided to open their own hospital. This group of black medical professionals that included dentists and pharmacists pooled their money and with the help of the NAACP, the Urban League and the Mother's milk fund collected $6000. With this seed money, the Society bought a Victorian house at 580 Frederick and turned it into a 37- bed medical facility. It was named Dunbar Hospital, in honor of one of America's most prominent poets, Paul Lawrence Dunbar.

Dunbar Hospital was not only a hospital, but also a training institution for black nurses. In 1932, it was moved from its original site on Frederick, now Frederick Douglas, to a larger facility at 3764 Brush Street at Illinois. It was renamed Parkside General Hospital. In 1962, Parkside General was condemned and forced out of existence by the Medical Center Redevelopment Center Project.

The building on Frederick changed hands several times before the City of Detroit acquired it as part of the urban renewal area. In 1979, two physicians bought the building for $3000 and thwarted the city's plans to demolish it. In that year, the old Dunbar Hospital building was placed on the National Registry of Historical

The Dunbar Hospital, 580 Frederick.

Dunbar Hospital Staff

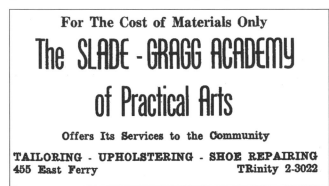

Places and a restoration costing in excess of $400,000 was begun. Much of the money raised for the project has come from the community. Today, Dunbar Hospital is a restored museum.

FAIRVIEW SANITARIUM

For decades, racial barriers had kept blacks from moving west of Beaubien, but in 1930, Dr. Greenidge broke the color line by founding the Fairview Sanitarium at 404-414 East Ferry, just east of Brush. It was founded in cooperation with two other physicians, Dr. Rupert Markoe and Dr. James Mc McClendon to treat patients who were not admitted at white hospitals.

Herman Kiefer was the hospital designated for many of the patients who had contracted tuberculosis. However, the tuberculosis epidemic that raged in the late 20's and early 30'ss overwhelmed Herman Kiefer's limited segregated facilities. This was a time when black physicians met with insurmountable difficulties in attempting to practice in white hospitals. Fairview was established as a hospital where black patients expected and received quality care and where doctors were greeted warmly and respectfully.

Dr. Greenidge headed Fairview until his death in 1966. The two buildings that housed Fairview Sanitarium have since been razed.

THE DETROIT MEMORIAL PARK CORPORATION

The Detroit Memorial Park Corporation was established in 1925 by a group of distinguished black Detroit businessmen to serve the Detroit's growing black population. The acknowledged founder was Charles Diggs, a mortician and Dr. Aaron Toodle, a pharmacist and first president. The corporation was housed in the Detroit Memorial Building at 446 East Warren. This was the address where one visited to purchase burial plots. The goal of the corporation was to provide reasonably priced and appropriately dignified burials to counteract the indignities and poor quality of service often received by the black community. At that time, there were no black-owned and operated businesses of its kind existing in Michigan.

Courtesy of Roberta Greenidge Hughes Wright

Dr. Robert I. Greenidge was one of three black physicians, who founded Fairview Sanitarium in 1930 to treat patients barred from white hospitals.

The cemetery itself is located at Thirteen Mile Road and Ryan Road in Warren, Michigan. It is the final resting place for many distinguished Detroiters, civic, professional and business leaders, including Elijah McCoy, the famous inventor. The founder, Charles Cole Diggs, Sr. and his son, Charles Jr. are buried in this cemetery. Detroit Memorial Park remains a viable cemetery for many in the black community. The cemetery has its own Michigan Historical Marker, registered and erected in 1976.

THE GREAT LAKES MUTUAL LIFE INSURANCE COMPANY

The Great Lakes Mutual Life Insurance Company evolved from a one room home office on Beacon Street during the depression that sold only five cents life insurance policy contracts to a company with twelve district offices in Michigan, in Ohio and in Washington D.C. By 1962, with Louis C. Blount at the helm, the company offered a full range of policies including the unborn child, educational endowments, mortgage insurance cancellations, special business contracts through Old Age.

Great Lakes also had a Federal Credit Union. The admitted assets were over nine million dollars and legal reserves were above seven and one-half million dollars. By 1962, Great Lakes had a new home office that spanned an entire block on Woodward Avenue between Euclid and Philadelphia with all modern facilities. Great Lakes provided employment and enjoyment for many hundreds with a Great Lakes Bowling Team, a Great Lakes Choir and a Great Lakes Teen-agers group who were at times, treated to travel and to cruises including a Hawaiian Cruise.

Their first President was Charles H. Mahoney. . Members of the Board of Directors were a virtual Who's Who of prominent black Detroiters with names as Alfred Pelham, Dr. DeWitt T. Burton, Dr. Robert L. Greenidge, Agnes Bristol and William Hanson. The original Board of Directors included Albert E. Finney, Moses Lionel Walker, Henry W. Holcomb, Everett Irving Watson and William C. Osby.

1934

THIRD HOME OFFICE
301 E. WARREN AVENUE
ENTIRE BUILDING

1945

FOURTH HOME OFFICE
82 E. HANCOCK AVENUE
ENTIRE BUILDING

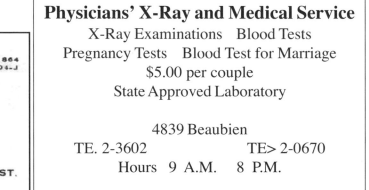

City Cab writes new chapter in Black history

THE MICHIGAN CITIZEN • DECEMBER 31ST, 2000 -

Photo by Jesse Leong-bey

By Jesse Long-Bey
The Michigan Citizen

More than 70 years ago, 38 years before Maulana Karenga created Kwanzaa, a group of African American taxi drivers and owners were practicing the Nguzo Saba. Their "Club House" was located at 706 Wilkins near Hastings Street, in the heart of Detroit's Paradise Valley. It was there on July 17, 1928 that they formulated plans for what has become, as City Cab proudly states, "this country's oldest African American owned and operated taxi company."

They were serious men who wanted to create an institution that would serve them and their people. Black Bottom, as Paradise Valley was also called, was be-

coming a thriving African American community. Black taxi drivers couldn't get work with white cab companies, and white drivers wouldn't pick up Black people.

So Louis Spann, Clifford Wiggins, Newton A. Dolphin, George I. Hutchinson; Arthur (Shaky) Norman, Eutha Hatcher, Timothy W. Johnson, Charles White, and H.B. Talaferro decided to do something about it.

They incorporated City Cab Company on July 31, 1928. The articles of incorporation were received, filed and approved by the Corporate Division of the Department of the State for the State of Michigan on August 3, 1928.

The company grew, adding new members; among them was Dora

Sanford in 1930, who became the first female cab owner/operator. City Cab Company and Victory Cab Company merged in 1930, and the operation was moved from the "Club House" on Wilkins Street to the corner of St. Antoine and Alfred.

Despite World War II, the company continued to grow and soon relocated to 583 E. Vernor Highway. The new facility had a larger repair shop, office, and dispatch area. Another merger occurred in 1957, when Wayne Overseas Cab and Courtesy Cab became a part of City Cab.

The company had to move again in 1965. Not because it needed more space, but because of urban renewal efforts in the city — which included the construction of the Fisher Freeway.

City Cab remained at

2541 Brush until February 1974, when it moved to its present location at 289 Adelaide.

There are 14 past presidents of City Cab Company. Ronald Baul is the current president of a company that has 350 cabs and 75 members. Baul says City Cab doesn't just do business in Detroit — it is an integral part of the community.

"Giving something back to the community isn't just a goal," Baul said. "It's an obligation."

The company offers scholarships to special needs children like those it has transported to and from school for over 30 years. To get to the polls on Election Day, a senior citizen need only call City Cab for a free ride there and back.

The company hasn't been without challenges. It

See Cab, Page A4

Orlin Jones / Collection

109

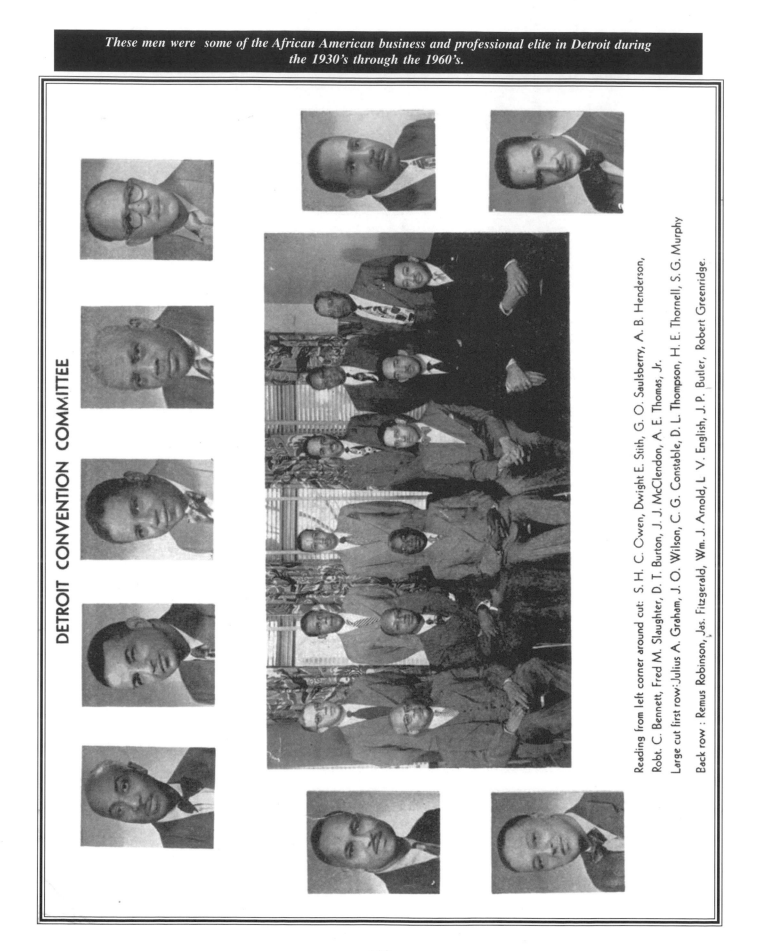

DETROIT CONVENTION COMMITTEE

Reading from left corner around cut: S. H. C. Owen, Dwight E. Stith, G. O. Saulsberry, A. B. Henderson, Robt. C. Bennett, Fred M. Slaughter, D. T. Burton, J. J. McClendon, A. E. Thomas, Jr.

Large cut first row: Julius A. Graham, J. O. Wilson, C. G. Constable, D. L. Thompson, H. E. Thornell, S. G. Murphy

Back row : Remus Robinson, Jas. Fitzgerald, Wm. J. Arnold, L V. English, J. P. Butler, Robert Greenridge.

The Carlton Plaza Hotel, on John R and Edmund Place, dates back to 1933. It Changed hands and became and became popular with African-Americans in October, 1949 after $500,000 worth of renovations.

FIRST ANNUAL

Commencement Exercise

OF

PORO OF DETROIT

APPROVED AND REGISTERED
SCHOOL OF BEAUTY CULTURE

Bethel A. M. E. Church
Detroit, Michigan
AUGUST 7th, 1936
8:30 P. M.

An Authorized Branch of
PORO COLLEGE INCORPORATED, CHICAGO
MRS. ANNIE M. MALONE, Founder and President

Office:
CAdillac 6539
CAdillac 3826

Dr. Wm. H. Lawson,   Dr. Wm. E. Lawson,
D.D., D.O.S.   D.D.
DR. WM. H. LAWSON
Michigan's First Registered Colored Optometris
With over 28 Years Experience
DR. WM. E. LAWSON
Optometrist and Optician
EYES EXAMINED   GLASSES FITTE
Offices: 1308 BROADWAY
At Gratiot, Room 202 Tobin Bldg., 2nd Floor

COMMUNITY MUSIC SCHOOL
Licensed by the Michigan Board of Education
Instruction in all Branches of Music and Dramatic Arts
Temple 2-0044   Temple 2-9536   268 -270 E. Forest, Detroit 1, Michigan

---

This photo of the staff of the Bee Dew Cosmetics Co. on East Forest — owned by Vivian Nash — is among hundreds the Charles H. Wright Museum of African American History will exhibit starting Saturday.

Randora Hotel - Owned by Randolph & Ora Belle Wallace

Randolph W. Wallace (above, left) owed and operated one of the first self-service grocery stores on the near Eastside. Pictured below are R. W. Wallace and Lester McMurtry, (1947).

113

Ben's Tire and Battery Service on East Forest..
(L to R) Johnie Weaver, Dallas, Uncle Benny and two unknown workers.

Abdul Muthleb making coffee - "Blue Goose" Restaurant, 4121 Hasting, Detroit, MI (1930's).

Lark's Drugstore on Beaubien

Chapter Seven
Our Entertainment
It Was Paradise... and Beyond

If you lived anywhere in the Detroit area and came to adulthood in the 20's, 30's, 40's or 50's, you will remember the names, Paradise Valley, Black Bottom, the Paradise Theater, the Flame and Frolic Show Bars, the Club El Sino, the 606 Horseshoe Lounge and the Club Three 666's. If you were lucky, you will have had the pleasure of visiting or frequenting all of some of these places or perhaps one of the many other clubs, bars, restaurants and hotels that were in existence during this time. These were the glory days on Detroit's Near East Side. It has been said that some few actually moved to Detroit in order to experience a level of black entertainment that was phenomenal and unprecedented in the black experience.

Those in the know, knew that Paradise Valley was a special kind of place, a legendary place with nightclubs and bars that rivaled the famous Harlem nightspots that have been showcased in such movies as "Harlem Nights" and "The Cotton Club." It was no paradise, this Paradise Valley, but one might say that it was a kind of Mecca that lured Detroiters and out-of-towners to it just as surely as bees flock to honey. One Near East Side member recalls vividly a Caucasian friend telling her how much and how many times he had wished he could have been a black man in Paradise Valley on a Saturday night. But one didn't need to be black to enjoy Paradise Valley or the nightclub scene on the Near Eastside. It was perhaps true that blacks had more fun but all one really needed for a really good time was a pocket full of dollars or perhaps just a fistful, and Paradise Valley was yours for the taking. In the thirties, forties, and yes, the fifties, this was one of the few areas of the city where whites and blacks could and did meet, mingle, and celebrate the special pleasures to be found in "The Valley" and on the Near East Side of Detroit.

When Dakota Staton sang of "Broadway" as a place where 'lights were brighter than day' and of 'sweethearts and beaus dressed up in their Sunday best clothes' she might well have been describing what could be found in Paradise Valley and along the John R corridor and the surrounding area, especially on the weekends. On the Near East Side, the weekends were an event. Detroiters dressed up in their finest to see and be seen in the many bars and clubs, as well as some of the restaurants and hotels. The bright neon lights that lined the streets were hard to resist for those looking for a good time. Professional men rubbed shoulders with the pimps, the factory workers and the numbers men. Suits could be either custom made or off the rack, just so long as the shoes were shiny. Outside of many bars and restaurants, shoeshine "boys" were busy plying their trade and making a living. Berry Gordy in his autobiography "To Be Loved" speaks of the days he made over $100 shining shoes outside of one of the drinking establishments. If there was a hierarchy, the "big numbers men" seemed somewhere near the top. This was an era in which rank seemed to matter little. What mattered most was your answer to the question, "How long and how green is your money and how much of it are you willing to spend?"

One may well ask, "What was it about Detroit and Detroiters that made this abundance of nightclubs, bars, restaurants and hotels on the Near Eastside possible?" The answers are many. Historically, even as slaves, blacks were a joyful people. When we had little or nothing, we sought and practiced a religion of hope. Through our songs, we 'made a joyful noise unto the lord'. In our more fundamentalist churches, we danced...Oh how we danced! Our Baptist church picnics were legendary for wholesome fun and the best food that black

people could put together. Even in times of privation, we feasted. Though we didn't eat 'high on the hog', we made our own feasts of every part of the pig that was available to us. Many of us still do. Still remembered are the words from a song black people used to sing, "We are happy people, yes we are." Black people may not have been as happy as this song suggests, but happiness was always one of our goals. When their economic situations improved, blacks moved to a larger world, one that allowed them to have a more hedonistic fun and to seek entertainment outside of their churches and families.

Some of the black Detroiters were descendants of slaves who had moved to the North and to Canada and back via the Underground Railroad. These scions had a leg up on their less sophisticated country cousins, the more recent arrivals from the South. These 'Old Detroiters' were more prosperous and were more likely to be employed as Pullman porters and Red Caps. They were the ones who had jobs on the ships that plied

Group Partying at Club Three 666

118

the Great Lakes ferrying iron ore and coal to run the Ford Rouge Foundry and the other steel making companies. They drove cabs and jitneys. They were among the first black entrepreneurs and professional people. Many owned homes and property. They invested in their businesses and families. They may have had more available cash, but they tended to use it more efficaciously than the factory workers did. Yet, the call of 'Saturday Night' was a lure few could resist. These "Old Detroiters" were happy to rub shoulders with the crowds that celebrated Saturday nights.

T. Bone Walker, Big Joe Turner and Bobby (Blue) Bland were among the many who sang "Stormy Monday Blues." The lyrics of this song really resonated with the crowds. These musicians understood what they were talking about when they sang, "Yes, the eagle flies on Friday, and Saturday night I go out to play." After a long week working at some of the most physically demanding, albeit fairly good paying jobs, black workers were ready for the proverbial wine, women and song. In fact, the weekend began on Thursday night for those automobile workers who worked the afternoon shift. They were paid on Thursday, and with cash in their pockets, it was party time as many of them went out to the clubs, bars and restaurants. These workers didn't have to drink or party alone. Women were out in force, not only the 'Ladies of the Evening' or the so called 'sporting women' but a bevy of women, young and old, attractive or not, seeking the same things that the men sought. They were eager to have a good time with those men who had the wherewithal and were willing to spend it on a good time.

There was a proliferation of bars and nightclubs in Paradise Valley and in Black Bottom in the 40's and 50's. Some of the popular clubs in the area included the Club Three Sixes and the 606 Horseshoe Bar on E. Adams, the Frolic Show Bar on John R and the El Sino on St. Antoine Street. Described here are a few of them.

The **Club El Sino** opened in 1947. William H. Pierce owned it. The El Sino was one of the very top entertainment venues in Paradise Valley. Della Reese, Sarah Vaughn and many other headliners performed there. What distinguished the Club El Sino from some of the other big clubs was the fact that the El Sino was an early purveyor of Modern jazz or Be-bop. Dizzy Gillespie's big band

Eugene Elzy and Ruperta Fleming at The Flame Showbar.

Younger sister of Freda Payne, lead singer for the Supremes 1973 - 1977.

Scherrie Payne

Billy Woods (far left) and Joe Louis with Greta Starks Party at The Flame Showbar.

was featured there. Charlie Parker's Quintet played there for two weeks in 1947. Illinois Jacquet and Gene Ammons provided entertainment there. Despite the proliferation of Modern Jazz or Be-bop, the El Sino retained the more familiar club characteristics with a large dance floor and two floor shows a night. The Club El Sino was the last of the famed clubs in Paradise Valley to close its doors, surviving until 1962.

The premier supper club of the 40's was the **Club Three 666** on East Adams. Entrepreneur Jap Sneed opened it in 1941. It was elegant with white linen tablecloths on each table, an unaccustomed nicety at the time. The food was reputed to be excellent. The clientele at lunchtime were the well dressed if not always well heeled who worked in the downtown area. Judging from the number of souvenir photos that abound, this was the club that most blacks were proud to be seen in. The entertainment was top notch. The shows included the big bands, the headliners as well as local musicians and a chorus line.

The most important and premier nightclub for entertainers and entertainment on the Near East Side in the 50's was the **Flame Show Bar**. In 1950, a non-black entrepreneur, Morris Wasserman, opened a very special nightclub located on the corner of Canfield and John R. It was a 'black and tan' club that played to a mixed race crowd seven nights a week. The shows were first rate, featuring a headliner, an exotic or "shake dancer" and a comedian. The Flame Show Bar was so popular and its shows were so highly regarded that customers would often form a line to get in that extended around the corner. At these times, 'greasing the palms' of the doorman was the only way to be assured entrance to a show. Every patron was given a pair of knockers upon admittance to the Flame. Patrons used these knockers in lieu of handclapping or perhaps along with it to rap on the tables, on the glasses, the bottles and anything suitable within their reach. It was a loud and joyful noise that was made! Dinah Washington, Sarah Vaughn, Billie Holiday and T Bone Walker were among the many headliners who performed at the Flame. When you wanted the best nightclub entertainment in Detroit, the Flame Show Bar is where you went. It was not a casual bar. When you visited the Flame, the bandleader,

First Nighters backstage at the Paradise Theater with Cab Calloway.

Mary Cooley

Freda Cooley

Mrs. Mary Cooley

Walter Duncan

Gladys Cooley

Paul Cooley

Coctail Party at The Carlton Plaza. Gladys Cooley, Hostess
New Orleans Suite, 1950.

Connie Dixon (in white hat) and Friends at Club Juana.

Maurice King sported a Tuxedo. The emcee, Ziggy Johnson, was always 'dressed to the nines.' So how could you be different? It was imperative that you looked good in *this* neighborhood. Black people have traditionally been 'style people' and in no place was this fact more evident than at the Flame Show Bar.

The **Garfield Lounge** near the corner of Garfield and John R. was notable among the many clubs and bars in the area. The very fun and almost posh Wal-Ha Room, an extension of the bar area, enhanced the popularity of the Garfield Lounge. The Garfield Lounge itself had no live entertainment. The patrons themselves were the entertainment. The Reverend C.L. Franklin of New Bethel Baptist Church held court at the lounge regularly with his group of hangers on and admirers. Formal entertainment could be found in the Wal-Ha Room. This was one of the mellowest places to drink, and on the occasion of "Chicken in the Basket" nights, one of the favorite places to eat. The Wal-Ha Room was where the young and beautiful people, the elites and the wannabes often frequented. The music was

classy. Most often, the gifted organist and pianist, Bob Wyatt, supplied the music. At other times there might be a trio providing music. The Wal-Ha room also featured some of the finest local jazz musicians. This was a classy place, due in large measure to the high standards of the owner, Randolph Wallace, a Mississippi transplant who began his business in Detroit with a small grocery store. As his business and resources grew, Mr. Wallace opened the Garfield Lounge and hotel and later, the Randora Hotel.

A tad further down on the list of great entertainment venues was the **Parrot Lounge and Bar** on the corner of Canfield and Beaubien. The entertainment at the Parrot was often, but not exclusively, local talent. The Parrot Bar was one of the early purveyors of jazz music and of the jazz musicians that were beginning to take their place on the world music stage. Located just off of the main drag, one might go to the Parrot if one either wished a little more privacy, did not wish to be seen out on the town or the jingle in the pocket was a little light. When you left the Parrot, you might

(Above, L to R) Walter Bailey, Katie Bailey, Mary Walker, Christ (CeeCee) Bray & Nelson Walker (Frolic Show Bar). (Below, L to R) Joyce Cranon, Unknown, Teola Cranon, Bob Gragg, Fay Hale, Billy Woods and Betty Bennett.

D. M. PENDLETON

Justine Rogers Wylie and William Miller at The Flame Showbar.

be inclined to buy hot tamales from the "Tamale Man" who stood on the corner until the streets quieted down at night. If you were very lucky, you might have a chance to buy the very best fried apple or peach pies in town from the "Pie Lady." Stanley's Mania was across the street from the Parrot Bar. Stanley's was reputed to have the best Chinese food in Detroit

Sportree's Music Bar on Hastings at Adams was one of the more popular bars. On one or more nights a week, patrons might find a show consisting of female impersonators or transvestites and either/ or vocalists and dancers. Sportree's was popular with some of the younger set because it had a more relaxed policy on age restrictions than did some nightspots. More than a few teens from the Near East Side of Detroit had their first nightclub experiences and their first bar drinks at Sportree's Music Bar. These neophyte drank "Pink Ladies" or Scotch with milk and Crème De Cacao that revealed their youth and inexperience with the bar scene.

Sunnie Wilson's Forest Club located at Forest Avenue and Hastings was a favorite for those who liked to drink as well as for those who simply wished to bowl or roller-skate. It was famous for its bar, allegedly the longest bar in Detroit. Sunnie Wilson's popularity was such that many celebrities and show people frequented the Forest Club during its heyday. This is the place where Joe Louis bowled. Sunnie Wilson's Forest Club was the place where Paul Robeson spoke in 1949. Young adults and teen-agers filled the skating rink on the weekends. The race riot of 1943 added a dimension of notoriety to the Forest Club when a rumormonger came to the Forest Club on that fateful June night and told the assembled patrons that white people had thrown a pregnant black woman off of the Belle Isle Bridge. The inflamed crowd of perhaps 500 took to the streets and began overturning cars, and decimating and looting white owned businesses. Thus the infamous riot began in earnest.

The Graystone Ballroom, billed as "Detroit's Million Dollar Ballroom" on Woodward Avenue near Canfield, was the most popular place for Detroiters to go dancing. It could accommodate 3000 customers on its floors and balconies.

Show Troupe in Front of Flame Showbar. Party includes Nellie Hill and Morris Wasserman, owner of the Flame Showbar (on bus), Ziggy Johnson (Emcee), Mantan Moreland, Maurice King (Bandleader) and Beans Bowles (saxophone player) (1952).

126

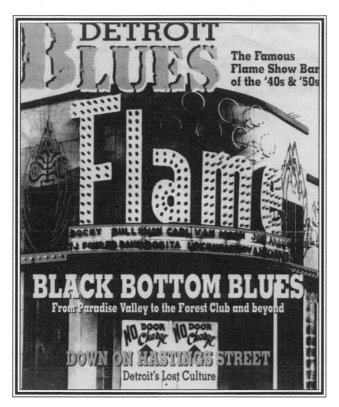

Teola Cranon with Sunnie Wilson, Owner of The Forest Club.

Monday was the day reserved for blacks to enjoy the Graystone although the ballroom was available whenever there was an open night. The NAACP, the Nacirima Club, the fraternities and the sororities, all held dances at the Graystone. On Mondays, the Graystone would come alive. This was not a casual or inexpensive place to dance where one just dropped in. There was an air of elegance about it. The best of the big bands played at the Graystone and the costs to be there were commensurate to the ambience of the building, the quality of the service and the music. Taxis would be lined up for blocks waiting to deposit the clientele, all dressed in their most splendid clothes and prepared to spend a lot of money, for the Graystone Ballroom was the fanciest and most expensive place to dance in Detroit. It was also the only major ballroom that regularly employed black bands and orchestras in the 1930's. By 1950, the Graystone Ballroom recognized the popularity of Modern Jazz and envisioned the possibility of teens and young adults dancing to this music. One memorable event in 1953 was billed as "The Battle of the Bands" with Charlie Parker's band battling the bands of Illinois Jacquet and Arnett Cobb.

The Arcadia Ballroom was another ballroom where black people were allowed to

frequent on occasion. It was located at 3527 Woodward at the corner of Stinson. Like the Graystone Ballroom, black people could obtain the Arcadia whenever there was an open night. It lacked the opulence of the Graystone Ballroom but was popular when attainable. The Arcadia was also popular with a few as a roller skating rink.

One could rave for hours about the "Valley " that was Paradise or the "Bottom" that was Black. However, Paradise Valley was not *all* Paradise. It was a place where dreams could be realized, shattered and then made new again. The streets were not paved with the proverbial gold, but with money that did not come only from the emerging middle class and the autoworkers. Paradise Valley and its environs were also places and streets where hustlers and pimps, gamblers, prostitutes and big "numbers men" frequented and where some plied their trades. The use of drugs was allegedly widespread among the big entertainers and their followers.

As African-American homes and businesses were demolished during the urban renewal era of the 1950's, so went the golden years of entertainment and business in the area s known as Black Bottom and Paradise Valley. There is an old axiom that says, "It is better to be a *has been* than a

(Above) Morris Wasserman and Mantan Moreland at The Flame Showbar. (Below) Ed Brazelton, legendaryy florist, with Nellie Hill, movie actress, beauty queen and headliner nightclub singer.

never was." Detroit *was*! There may never be an entertainment district in Detroit as fabulous as Black Bottom or Paradise Valley, but these were glorious days in Detroit, heady days that will not be forgotten as long as those who lived those days retain memory.

———

Club B & C
Paradise Valley's Original
THEATER BAR
CL-1730   1730 St. Antoine
INAUGURATES A NEW
COCKTAIL HOUR
FOR DOMESTICS
Starting January 22nd
Every Thursday
Floor Show at 7:00 P.M.
Choice Wine - Beers - Whiskey
Finest Entertainment in
PARADISE VALLEY

GARFIELD LOUNGE
John R. Corner of Garfield

(Above) Cynthia Braithwaite (far right) and friends at The Garfield.
(Below, L to R) Edgar Lawrence, Anna Carter, Robert Searcy and Dorothy ? at the 606 Horseshoe Lounge.

Chapter Eight
The Detroit
Police Department

By John Henry & Joynal A. Muthleb

The intent of this chapter is to highlight the contributions that black police officers who resided on the Near Eastside made against many odds to the Detroit Police Department and to the City of Detroit.

The police officers mentioned and profiled in this chapter endured many forms of discrimination and abuse as black men working in a racially segregated Police Department. These exceptional, courageous officers patrolled the streets of the city (particularly the Near Eastside) and distinguished themselves in the performance of their duties. The majority of the black police officers were patrolmen.

The Detroit Police Department was established on March 12, 1861. The first uniformed police officers were deployed on the streets of Detroit in 1865. There were no black police officers in the Detroit Police Department from 1865 to 1878.

On May 6, 1878, John A Wilson, a black man, was appointed to the Detroit Police Department. Four years after his appointment, Officer Wilson was dropped from the Department (February 15, 1882).

The second black man, Joseph Stowers was appointed to the Department on April 10, 1890. Officer Stowers was not confirmed and was dropped from the Department.

On July 16, 1895, George Carmichael was appointed to the Department. He became the first black to retire from the Detroit Police Department on October 1, 1924.

Warren C. Richardson, a "Near Eastsider," was appointed to the Detroit Police Department on

William C. Richardson

March 31, 1900. Officer Richardson was the first black police officer to attain the rank of Detective Sergeant. Officer Richardson retired in 1926 as a Detective Sergeant.

Daniel O. Smith joined the Detroit Police Department in 1901. Officer Smith was appointed to Detective Sergeant in 1914, and Detective Lieutenant in 1927. Officer Smith retired in 1932. Officer Smith became the Department's first black Detective Lieutenant.

On April 28, 1921, *Grayce Murphy* became the first black female appointed to the Detroit Police Department.

Early promotions of black police officers often occurred in the Detective Division. This practice would limit their authority to a small number of black subordinate officers. One has to keep in mind that black officers suffered the same indignities that the black citizens of Detroit endured.

A clear example of the discriminatory practices directed toward black officers can be illustrated by the attempts of Officer *Jessie Stewart,* a "Near Eastsider," to earn a promotion to Uniform Sergeant. Officer Stewart joined the Detroit Police Department in December 1940. Officer Stewart had earned a degree from the University of Michigan. In the nineteen forties, it was difficult for a black officer to earn a promotion to Uniform Sergeant. Stewart took the promotional exam for Uniform Sergeant on several occasions. He placed number one on the promotional list and police officials began making promotions from the number two position, totally ignoring the fact that Officer

Stewart was entitled to be promoted before any other officer. On another occasion, Officer Stewart placed second on the promotional list for Uniform Sergeant. Police officials then promoted the white police officer in the number one position, skipped over Officer Stewart and promoted white officers beneath his second place position on the promotional list. When Officer Stewart inquired why he hadn't been promoted, the ranking officials informed him that he had a "bad attitude." Officer Stewart's "bad attitude'" in fact, was his unrelenting and persistent efforts to seek equal treatment for black police officers.

Officer Stewart was a positive role model for fellow police officers. Officer Stewart's personal "struggle against all odds" finally produced results. He was eventually promoted to Uniform Sergeant and retired at that rank on May 15th, 1966.

There were only 39 black police officers in 1940. This represented 1% of the entire Police Department. Through the efforts and recommendations of several black political and social organizations, the mayors of the City of Detroit made half-hearted efforts to hire more black police officers. By 1952, the Police Department had 118 black officers, 3% of the entire department.

In January 1946, *Lawrence Johnson* became the first black Uniform Sergeant. In 1955, there were six black Uniform Sergeants, Lawrence Johnson, James Leigh, Jesse Stewart, Harry Nutall, George Harge and George Scott. Sergeants Johnson, Leigh and Stewart were assigned to the Hunt Street Station (Third Precinct). Sergeant Nutall was assigned to the cellblock, (1st Precinct). Sergeant Harge was assigned to the city wide Vice Bureau and Sergeant Scott was assigned to the 13th precinct. Most of the black patrolmen were usually assigned to the Third (Hunt Street), the ninth (Bethune) or the Thirteenth (Woodward) precincts.

On November 6, 1950, *Frank A. Blount,* a "Near Eastsider," was appointed to the Detroit Police Department. Officer Blount's intense interest in unbiased effective

Jessie Stewart

132

law enforcement, his work ethic, and subsequent education enabled him to achieve the rank of Executive Chief of the Detroit Police Department.

During his career in law enforcement, Officer Blount earned his B.S. and M.S. Degrees in Criminal Justice from Wayne State University, studied a year at Harvard University as a "Fellow", and studied at Michigan State University's School of Labor and Industrial Relations. Officer Blount recognized the need for an organization for black police officers. The Detroit Police Officers Association (DPOA) at that time did not adequately or fairly represent black police officers. This motivated Officer Blount and several other black police officers to form an organization of black law enforcement officers called "The Guardians." Officer Blount was also a founding member of the " National Organization of Black

Frank Blount

Law Enforcement Executives," (NOBLE), a member of "The Lieutenants and Sergeants Association," a private investigator (State of

Michigan) and a member of "The Retired Detroit Police and Firefighter's Association."

Throughout his career as a Police Officer and Executive, Frank Blount earned the respect of the rank and file policemen (Black and White) by the unbiased, fair, and honest way that he treated his fellow officers. After Frank Blount retired on April 1, 1977, he served as Chief of Security for the Detroit Public Schools from 1978-1989. Officer Blount's career, as it was with all black policemen, was truly " a struggle against all odds."

Another "Near Eastsider" involved in " struggle against all odds" was Officer *John Henry*. In 1954, before he joined the Detroit Police Department, the Chicago Cubs Baseball Team recruited John Henry from the "Ford All-star Nine" which was a part of the Detroit Baseball Federation Class A Division. John Henry was often described as a flashy, hard hitting third baseman

John Henry was assigned to the Cubs' Minor League. He played third base for the Janesville Farm Team in the Wisconsin State Minor League system. John returned to Detroit in 1955 and joined the Detroit Police Department on June 6th of that year. Henry worked at the First Precinct. He was assigned to a scout car and patrolled the downtown area of the city. Occasionally, he worked with the Precinct Vice Squad. In his vice squad activities, Officer Henry was very effective. The Inspector of the City-wide Narcotics Bureau recognized Officer Henry's skills as a precinct Vice Squad Officer and Officer Henry was assigned as an investigator with the Bureau.

In July of 1968, Officer Henry was promoted to Sergeant. Five years later, he was promoted to Lieutenant. In March 1976, Mayor Coleman Young appointed Lieutenant Henry to Inspector. In the following years, 1978 to 1983, Inspector Henry was rapidly promoted to Commander and Deputy Chief. Henry retired from the Police Department on December 31, 1993 as a Deputy Chief. On January 2, 1994, Henry was appointed Executive Director of the Detroit Police Athletic League. As Executive

John Henry

As a police officer, Percy Hart received several citations for valor. Officer Hart's desire to fight the racism that existed in the police department motivated him to seek a position as a Union Steward in the Detroit Police Officers Association. Percy was the first Black Union Steward for the Detroit Police Officers Association. (D.P.O.A.) Officer Hart was an effective voice for Black policemen.

Officer Hart enjoyed working with children. When he was assigned to the Traffic Safety Division, Officer Hart effectively taught and entertained school children about traffic safety by using ventriloquism as and a dummy named "Leroy." Officer Hart retired after twenty-five years of service. Throughout his years of service, Officer Hart continued his "struggle against all odds."

Joynal A Muthleb, a "Near Eastsider," was appointed to the Detroit

Director, John Henry was responsible for more than eleven athletic programs and two multi purpose recreation centers. Under the Executive Director's leadership, the Police Athletic League gave City of Detroit youth, positive and constructive after school and weekend activities in a variety of sports. The Police Athletic League continues to provide a unique opportunity for the teenage participants to have a positive interactive relationship with Detroit Police Officers. John Henry retired from the Police Department on September 11, 1995.

Percy L. Hart, a "Near Eastsider," joined the Detroit Police Department on May2, 1952. Before he joined the police department, Officer Hart graduated from Northern High School, and attended Wayne State University. During World War 11, Percy Hart had been a "Waist Gunner" on a B-52 as a member of the United States Air Force. After he was honorably discharged from the Air Force in 1946, the Detroit Street Railway System hired him as a bus driver.

Percy Hart

Percy Hart and "Leroy"

From the records of the NAACP, January 1, 1956 through November 30, 1960, there were 149 police brutality complaints filed by black citizens in Detroit. Fifty-three of these complaints were the result of beatings received in precinct stations; forty-seven resulted in hospitalizations; fifty-one were cases referred to the police department for action. There were four cases in which the police department admitted wrongdoing.

Believe it or not, these figures were an improvement over previous years.

Officer Muthleb was a police officer for almost ten years. Officer Muthleb resigned from the Detroit Police Department in October 1960. Subsequently, Muthleb he began a career as a fully certified Special Education Teacher with the Detroit Public Schools.

In December of 1960, the United States Commission on Civil Rights subpoenaed Mr. Muthleb to give testimony regarding violations of the Civil Rights Act relative to the Detroit

Police Department on June 18, 1950. Officer Muthleb had extensive experience walking a beat, scout car duty, and "special assignments" as an officer in the City -wide Vice Bureau.

In the early 1950's, there were few promotions of black police officers. The seniority of black officers was usually ignored when it involved specialized assignments. White police officers with less seniority than black police officers were assigned to scout cars and black officers were assigned to foot patrol.

There were many incidents that Officer Muthleb and other black officers witnessed. There were frequent incidents of selective law enforcement specifically directed toward the *black community* by white police officers and many incidents of unnecessary force used to effect an arrest.

Joynal A. Muthleb

Police Department. Mr. Muthleb's testimony covered his experiences as a Detroit Police Officer the area of police brutality against black citizens in the City of Detroit, discrimination by the Detroit Police Department against black police officers, discrimination against the civil rights of black citizens of Detroit, the negative attitude of the Detroit Police Department toward anti-discrimination laws and Mr. Muthleb's personal experiences as a minority police officer subject to the discriminatory practices of the Detroit Police Department.

Mr. Muthleb's testimony before the National Civil Rights Commission was published in "Hearings before The United States Commission on Civil Rights." Hearings held in Detroit, Michigan December 14 and December 15, 1960. Detroit helped to modify the racist, discriminatory attitudes and practices that existed in the Detroit Police Department.

Nathaniel Carr, a "Near Eastsider," joined the Detroit Police Department on September 22, 1947. During his service as a police officer, Carr earned a degree in Industrial Engineering from the Lawrence Institution of Technology in 1958. Officer Carr was able to earn his degree by attending school on his off days. After serving as a police officer for seventeen years, Officer Carr resigned from the Detroit Police Department to pursue a career as an engineer with the Chrysler Corporation. Carr worked at the Chrysler Corporation's Stamping Plant and Missile Defense Plant. When he retired from the Chrysler Corporation, Mr. Carr continued to work as a Consultant Engineer at the Army Tank Automotive Command. Mr. Carr earned a reputation for his outstanding work in research and development. Nathaniel Carr's activities as a police officer for the City of Detroit, as an engineer for the Chrysler Corporation, a Colonel in the U.S. Army Reserves, a Tuskegee Airman and his many volunteer efforts in local Detroit organizations truly exemplified his "struggles against all odds."

Collins Glenn, a " Near Eastsider," joined the Detroit Police Department on October 20, 1947. Officer Glenn possessed unique leadership qualities

Nathaniel Carr

that made him popular with his fellow police officers and with command personnel. Because of Officer Glenn's knowledge of street patrol and scout car duty, many officers sought his advice and counsel relative to their duties as police officers. Officer Glenn's fellow officers considered it a privilege to work and to be tutored by him. Later in his police career, Officer Glenn was transferred from street duty to the Court detail. As a Court official, he was a definite asset to the court system.

Officer Glenn retired from the Police Department on October 4, 1974. After his retirement, the "Friend of the Court" hired Officer Glenn to work for them at the state level. His duties involved the apprehension of individuals who were delinquent in paying their child support obligations. His job required that he travel throughout the State of Michigan.

Throughout his police career, Officer Glenn always welcomed police officers into his home. Many officers frequented the Glenn household to socialize and to swap stories about their on the job police experiences. Officer Glenn's "struggle against all odds" sets a positive example for black officers.

Leo Gleaton, a "Near Eastsider," joined the Detroit Police Department on September 22, 1947. In his twelve-year police career, Officer Gleaton was a " walking textbook" on effective street patrol and scout car duty. He had an unusual approach in making an arrest or mediating family disputes. His calm demeanor and smooth talk usually eliminated potential violence that could erupt while effecting an arrest.

Officer Gleaton was sensitive to the racial discrimination that he experienced as a member of the Detroit Police Department. However, he was acutely sensitive to the discriminatory attitudes of the citizens he was sworn to protect. On more than one occasion, Officer Gleaton and his partner would respond to a radio run to "assist a citizen." On one occasion when Officer Gleaton confronted the

Leo Gleaton

complainant, the response from the complainant was," Why are you here? I want the *real* police." The complainant, a black woman, did not consider black police officers as bona fide policemen! The attitude displayed by this woman did not deter Officer Gleaton and his partner from making the proper disposition of the complainant. However, her attitude reflected how some black citizens perceived black police officers.

Officer Gleaton resigned from the Detroit Police Department on September 25, 1949 to pursue a new career in Los Angeles, California.

Collins Glenn

Wings Over Jordan

The Detroit —Fire Department—

The Detroit Fire Department was established by the Legislature of the City of Detroit in 1867. Prior to 1867, fire protection and fire fighting was carried out by volunteer citizens.

In the late 19th century and the early 20th century, fire engines were horse drawn.

Throughout these early years, there were no black firemen. It wasn't until 1938 that the first two black men, Marcena Taylor and Marvin White were hired by the City of Detroit. Joe Burell was hired as the third black in the Fire Department. In 1984, Charlie Steele was hired.

These men were subjected to the same patterns of discrimination and departmental prejudices that other pioneering black Americans faced when they were the first to break down racial barriers.

The Fire Department's promotional system was based on a strict seniority system. Because of the late hiring of blacks in this established seniority system, promotions could not occur for many years. When black firemen became eligible for promotion, their seniority was ignored.

It wasn't until Mayor Coleman Young initiated an affirmative action program that black firemen began to enjoy the benefits of the promotion system. Mayor Young appointed Melvin Jefferson, Sr. as the Fire Commissioner in 1988. Mayor Dennis Archer appointed Harold Watkins as Fire Commissioner. Both Appointments were the highest civilian positions in the Fire Department.

In the following years, black firemen continued their rapid rise in rank within the Detroit Fire Department.

"I wasn't allowed to eat with the other firemen."
— Marcena Taylor

Civil Defense volunteers pose with then-Sgt. Marcena Taylor in front of Engine Co. 34's quarters in the early 1950s.

Free Press file photo

Free Press file photo
Marcena Taylor, one of the first black firefighters in Detroit and the first to make battalion chief, in front of Engine Co. 34 after his retirement.

Diversity

Integrating the Detroit Fire Department was hard work. When Marcena lor reported for his first day of work, a small riot broke out. Taylor was one of the first black men hired by the department. The arrival of Taylor and anther black rookie one morning in 1938 brought out about 200 angry neighbors who blocked the entrance to the engine house on Livernois near Warren. The standoff lasted for hours until police dispersed the mob and allowed Taylor to start a career that lasted 33 years, culminating in his being named the department's first black battalion chief in 1969.

"I wasn't allowed to eat with the other firemen," Taylor recalled in a 1988 interview. "I wasn't allowed to use the bathroom facilities. I wasn't allowed to sleep in the same room."

It took 10 years for the fire union to make him a member. Taylor retired in 1971 and died in 1994.

The Detroit Fire Department is unusual among big-city departments in that members rise through the ranks by seniority only. In other words, firefighters' promotions to sergeant, lieutenant, captain and chief are governed by the retirements or deaths of members who joined the department before them. In other large departments, seniority is not the only factor. Promotions are based on test scores, other measurements of merit, politics — and how long a firefighter has been on the job.

Detroit Free Press

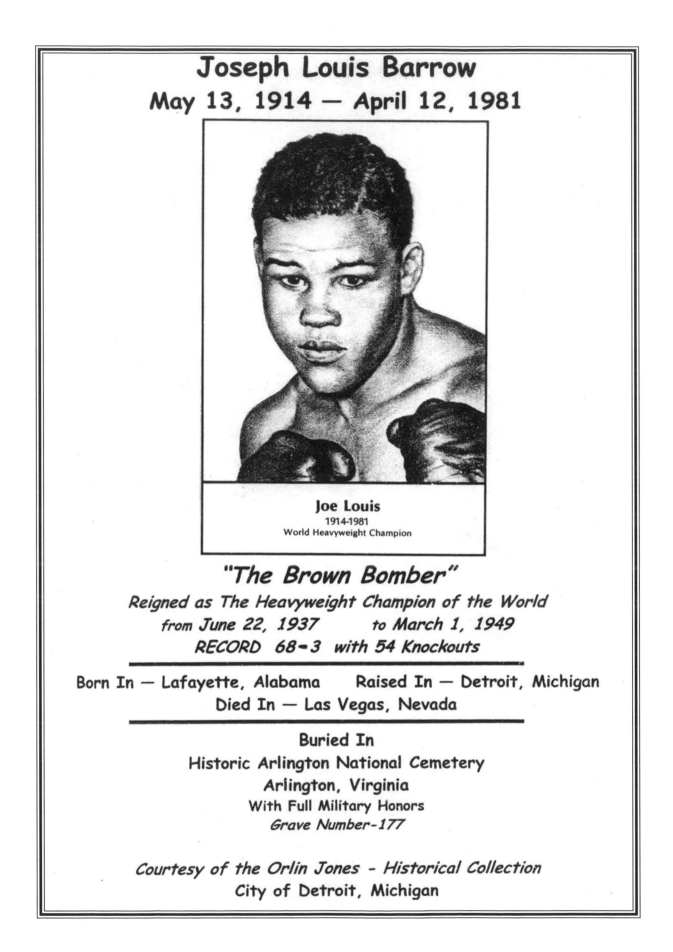

Joseph Louis Barrow
May 13, 1914 — April 12, 1981

Joe Louis
1914-1981
World Heavyweight Champion

"The Brown Bomber"
Reigned as The Heavyweight Champion of the World
from *June 22, 1937*   to *March 1, 1949*
RECORD *68-3 with 54 Knockouts*

Born In — Lafayette, Alabama   Raised In — Detroit, Michigan
Died In — Las Vegas, Nevada

Buried In
Historic Arlington National Cemetery
Arlington, Virginia
With Full Military Honors
Grave Number-177

Courtesy of the Orlin Jones - Historical Collection
City of Detroit, Michigan

Chapter Nine
Detroit's Sports History

With Contributions by Dr. John Kline aka "Jumping Johnny Kline"

Detroit's history of black Americans in sports is but a microcosm of the history of blacks in sports in the United States Although Detroit has had and continues to have its share of illustrious sports figures, today these athletes follow a path that had been smoothed of much of the racism that made this road so difficult to travel. As we talk about sports in Detroit, we have included a little of the history of sports that the younger generations have not experienced, but that the elders know too well.

There are few people in this country who have not heard of Joe Louis, popularly known as "The Brown Bomber." As fabulous as his career was, Louis was not the first heavyweight champion. At a time when blacks were barred from most professional sports, black men were making boxing history. This was one of the few sports where the black man's strength and agility were unquestioned. The legendary boxer, Jack Johnson, was the most applauded and perhaps the most gifted frontrunner as the first black man to win the

BUICK: Looking Ahead to the Second Century

A tradition of class and reliability continues

World heavy-weight champ and boxing legend Joe Louis is pictured by his brand-new 1935 Buick.

heavyweight crown in 1908. It was apparently not so difficult for whites to accept the 'brutish' strength of blacks. As for the other sports, the more 'cerebral' sports, acceptance of black men and women as equal professional participants was more problematical.

Let us look back to a time when there were no black professional basketball players in the United States. Until 1950, colleges and universities in the South were forbidden to have black-white team sports due to Jim Crow Laws. The American Basketball Association was formed in 1925, but black players were not allowed to join. Until 1937, there were no black college players in this city or in many cities in America. There was a time when there were no black "professional" baseball players nor tennis players or golf pros in this country. Since the days when blacks were excluded from most professional sports, there has been a giant leap forward. Jackie Robinson was the first black player in major league baseball, but he was not the first black player to become a baseball legend. Satchel Paige was, arguably, the best pitcher of his time, but he was no anomaly. The Negro Baseball League had many players who were world-class players and would have excelled in any league had they been given the chance. Satchel Paige gained notoriety in the Negro Baseball League as a pitcher without equal. Had Paige been allowed to play in the major leagues in his prime, he would have rivaled or beaten the best the American and National Leagues had to offer.

When we speak of basketball, our minds may go immediately to a current basketball icon, perhaps Shaquille O'Neil or possibly back to Kareem Abdul Jabbar or Oscar Robertson. These men followed a trail in professional basketball that had been made smooth by many others, most notably the first black men to play in the NBA, Chuck Cooper of the Boston Celtics or Earl Lloyd of the Washington Capitals. At the time when black men were denied entry as competitors into professional basketball, the world famous Harlem Globetrotters were organized. The strength, the agility and the ability of the Harlem Globetrotters to play *their* game of basketball, amazed fans throughout the world, and forced white "professional" teams,

coaches and owners to take another look at the talent they were foregoing because of racial barriers. The fifties marked the beginning of big changes for black basketball players. Today, blacks are the predominant players in the NBA. They not only play the game, they coach, manage and own NBA teams.

In 1951, trailblazer Althea Gibson broke the racial barrier at Wimbledon. Gibson was what African-Americans used to call a "First." Five years later, she became the first black woman to win a major tennis crown by winning the French championship title. In 1957, Gibson became the first black to win the Wimbledon women's singles title. Althea cemented her fame by winning the U.S. National championship at Forest Hills. Gibson was only permitted to play and compete in the American Lawn Tennis Association after winning a string of titles in the all-black American Tennis Association. It is difficult to imagine world-class tennis today without the Williams sisters, Venus and Serena.

Black Americans have been a dominant force in track and field for many years and for many reasons. Some attribute the preponderance of blacks in track and field to the time when black Africans had a need to run long distances to other villages at a swift pace. Others say that it is because the ability to jump and run was a way of life for black Americans, descendants of slaves, who wished to demonstrate their skill and ability on American soil. Participation in track and field events required sponsors and practice fields. Black athletes were required to seek their own sponsors if they wished to participate. Most of the sponsors of African-American athletes came from all-black secondary schools, black colleges and YMCA's.

John Baxter "Doc" Taylor was the first African-American Olympic gold medal winner when he competed in the 200-200-400-800 meter medley relays held in London, England in 1908. Howard Porter Drew from Lexington, Kentucky was called "The World's Fastest Human" when he ran the 100 meter dash in 10.8 seconds and the 70-yard dash in 7.5 seconds. Eddie Tolan won a Gold Medal in the 1932 Olympics in the 100-meter yard dash. Later, Jesse Owens won four gold medals in the 1936 Olympics in Berlin, Germany.

Joe Louis Retaliates Against Max Schmeling March 5, 1938.

Today, track and field events remain a strong, if not *the* strongest participatory sport for African-Americans.

JOE LOUIS BARROW, OR "THE BROWN BOMBER"

Detroit natives remember Joe Louis for many reasons. First and foremost are doubtless his exploits in the boxing ring. Joe Louis was one of the greatest boxers of all time, ending his professional career with a 68-3-0 record. When Max Schmeling hit the mat in the first round of the heavyweight championship bout 1937 following a vicious pummeling by Joe Louis, he hit it with a thud heard around the world. Those who recall that day remember the joy that pervaded the black community as residents paraded down streets blowing horns and whistles, beating drums, and singing "Joe knocked Schmeling out in the first round" to the tune of "Flat Foot Floogie," Joe not only redeemed himself for an earlier loss to Schmeling, but on that day, he bestowed or rekindled a sense of pride in black Americans that has had far- reaching implications to this day.

Joe's legacy is enhanced by his generosity to the black community from whence he came. Under-educated himself, Joe Louis often visited black schools, encouraging young people to excel. Joe gave money to poor children and to friends from his youth. He started a softball team, the Brown Bombers, and supported the team by providing uniforms, equipment and a bus for the team travel. Joe not only bought businesses, but also invested in friend's businesses. One such was Brown Bomber's Chicken Shack that flourished for a while at 424 East Vernor Highway. In 1940, Joe bought a farm in Utica for the horses he loved to ride. Everyone who was *anyone* in Detroit at that time *had* to visit Joe Louis's Farm and ride the horses that the farm rented out. This was one of the more popular places to be seen, to ride horses and to drink and dine at the well-appointed clubhouse.

The Joe Louis Fist that stands at the foot of Woodward Avenue may be the most graphic reminder of Joe's legacy. One may think, also, of the hockey arena that bears his name in the Cobo Hall complex or reflect upon Joe's statue that reposes in front the Detroit's city Hall. But for those who lived during Joe's reign, he is remembered as being "richer than a king;" a boxer whose purses in the first year and a half as a pro added up to $371,633 at a time when the average yearly salary was $1,250. Joe was tall and handsome, wildly successful and famous. He had a beautiful wife in Marva Trotter. Joe went places and did things that no black man in the United States had ever experienced so completely. His life was the stuff movies were made of and that a movie *was* made of. Coleman Young eulogized Joe Louis with these words, "He stood for everything that was good about Detroit." The Reverend Jesse Jackson added, "He was our Samson, our David." Perhaps these are Joe's truest and most abiding legacies.

NORMAN "TURKEY" STEARNES

One of baseball's greatest players, a Tennessee native by birth but a Detroiter by choice, was Norman "Turkey" Stearnes. "Turkey" was the nickname given to Stearnes because he ran the bases like a turkey, head bobbing and arms flapping. Like most black players of his times, Stearnes was underrated and unappreciated. Stearnes played baseball with the Detroit Stars of the Negro Baseball League from 1923 to 1931 as an extraordinary outfielder and a southpaw slugger who could not only hit and field but could run with blazing speed. He ended his first year in Detroit with a batting average of .365 and 17 home runs.

From 1933 to 1935, playing ball for the Chicago American Giants, Stearnes hit .342, .374,

and .430 respectively. In 1932, he led the Negro Southern League in doubles, triples, home runs and stolen bases, a feat that no major league player has ever accomplished. When Stearnes' active baseball career ended in 1941, he had a collection of trophies that included three batting championships, and six home run crowns. After baseball life ended, Stearns returned to Detroit to live. In the intervening years, he married a Detroit schoolteacher and worked at Ford Motor. He remained a Detroit resident until his death in 1979 at the age of seventy- eight years. Considered by many as the best black player in Detroit's baseball history, Norman "Turkey" Stearnes was inducted into the Baseball Hall of Fame at Cooperstown in the year 2000.

Turkey Stearnes poses with a baseball bat.

David Dombrowski, Tigers president, CEO and general manager stands next to Nettie Stearnes at Comerica Park in Detroit on Friday July 20, 2007. Next to them is the plaque honoring Nettie's late husband and Negro League baseball player Norman "Turkey" Stearnes.

BERTHA CRAIG, QUEEN OF DETROIT TENNIS

Bertha Craig moved to Detroit in 1920, attended Miller High School, and graduated from Northeastern High School in 1928. Bertha was an outstanding athlete. She played on the hockey, basketball, track and swimming teams. At Northeastern, Craig broke the record for the 75-yard dash. She also participated in the 550-yard dash and what was then called the obstacle hurdles. After high school, Craig played basketball and softball at Brewster Center, now Wheeler Center. Her softball team beat Hamtramck for the city championship in 1932.

Encouraged by her employer at Sweets Drug Store to play tennis at Belle Isle, Craig excelled at the game. She joined the tennis club at the Lucy Thurman YWCA and began to play in inter-city tournaments between Chicago, Cleveland and Detroit. Craig won the Midwest tournament in Louisville, Kentucky in 1949 and 1950. She also won three Midwest doubles tournaments with partner, Darnella Emerson. Her last tournament was a doubles match when Craig was more than 60 years old. Today, Craig remains physically active. She dances, sings, and walks at he Williams Recreation Center on Rosa Parks Boulevard. Bertha Craig is not only a legend in her own time, but truly a legend in Detroit sports.

Tennis Legend, Bertha Craig Toasted by Her Husband.

Bobby "SHOWBOAT" HALL, GLOBETROTTER PHENOMENON

It has been said that any Globetrotter who has played with "Showboat" Hall considers him to be the greatest Globetrotter, superior to the great Globetrotter showmen, Goose Tatum and Meadowlark Lemon.

"Showboat's personality and showmanship was so dominant that at times, he controlled the flow of play," alleges John Kline, Ph.D., himself a former Globetrotter. Kline says Detroit has produced more Globetrotters than any other city and Bobby Hall was probably the greatest Globetrotter to come out of the city. Hall played with the Globetrotters for 25 years and according to Globetrotters owner, Mannie Jackson, "He was one of the most respected to ever wear the Globetrotter's red, white and blue."

Hall was an all-around athlete at Miller High School, but he honed his basketball skills at Brewster Center, now Wheeler Center on Detroit's East Side. During Hall's career with the Globetrotters, he played in more than 5000 games and in 90 countries. Hall was both player and coach from 1968 until his retirement in 1974. Though the skillful use of his feet on the basketball court earned him the moniker "showboat" and prompted many laughs, Hall was a man of principles that garnered him respect as a player and as a team member.

Bobby Hall has retired from his position with the Wayne County Corrections Department and lives in Detroit with his wife, Kitty.

———

DR. JOHN KLINE AKA 'JUMPIN' JOHNNY KLINE

John Kline, a native Detroiter, has always been an amazingly multi-talented athlete whose talents began surfacing in his teen years. In the 1950's, within the short span of 15 months, Kline achieved four major milestones; he was named basketball All-American, voted MVP in the first Motor City Tournament in Detroit, voted 1952 Wayne State University Athlete of the Year, and achieved finalist status in the United States Olympic Trials in Track. While a student at Wayne State, Kline became known for playing basketball more like a professional than a college athlete so he made the difficult decision to place his college career on hold to trot around the world as a Harlem Globetrotter.

Kline was Wayne State's high-jumping ace and his high-jumping ability earned him the name. "Jumping Johnny Kline." In 1951 he broke Wayne's indoor and outdoor track records with a leap of 6 ft. 7 inches. Kline also excelled in the broad jump and the hop step for which his record jump qualified him for the Olympic finals in Los Angeles. In all, Kline holds three track records, unbroken to this day.

Kline started playing organized basketball at the Brewster Recreation Center at Brewster and Hastings Street in Detroit in 1949. Brewster Center was "the place" for sports and also a hub for social life in the black community in the 30's, 40's and 50's. The most talented ball players from around the city demonstrated their skills at Brewster Center. Kline played at Wayne State and at the same time, played for coach Gus Finney. Each year that he played at Brewster, his team won the league championship.

Still active, Dr. John Kline continues to lead the Youth Athletic Enrichment Program, an after school program which he developed and implemented 19 years ago. This is a program crafted in such a way that it attracts students through athletics, yet has its roots in academic enrichment. Kline organized the Black Legends of Professional Basketball Foundation to bring

"Jumping Johnny Kline" as a Harlem Globetrotter

Eddie Tolan

together and to recognize black professional black basketball players, now in their seventies and eighties who played basketball for the barnstorming teams from 1900-1960, before blacks could aspire for the NBA.

_____

Eddie Tolan, Olympic Gold Medal Winner

Eddie Tolan had been a football star at Cass Technical High school before he entered the University of Michigan in 1927, Tolan's selection from the seven schools which had attempted to recruit him. He found that the university was not ready for a football player on the freshman team, let alone a quarterback, his hoped for position, but learned that it was acceptable to join the track team. Tolan entered the track and field arena with a vengeance. Nicknamed "Midnight Express," Tolan set a national record in the 100-yard dash and tied the record in the 100-meter dash. He won the National Collegiate Athletic Association championship in the 200 and 220-yard dashes and the Amateur Athletic Union Championship in the

100 and 220-yard dashes between 1931 and 1932. Although Tolan was second to Ralph Metcalf in the 1932 Olympic trials for the Olympic games in Los Angeles in 1932, he bested Ralph Metcalf in the 100-meter with a world record 10.3 seconds. Eddie Tolan was the first black athlete to win an Olympic gold medal and the only American to win two medals in that year. In his life, Tolan won 300 races and lost only seven.

Tolan became a Detroit schoolteacher and volunteer coach for the Murray Wright Track team. He was named to the Michigan Sports Hall of Fame in 1958. He died in 1967 at the age of 58. Tolan was honored posthumously as one of University of Michigan's all-time greatest athletes.

_____

Charles and John Roxborough

Charles and John Roxborough were brothers who were the first black varsity players in the Detroit Public Schools. They played at Eastern High School from 1906-1910. They were stars on the team when Eastern won the city and state championships. Charles played center with the Detroit Spaulding basketball team during 1910 and 1911 and may be the first African-American professional basketball player from Detroit.

Charles Roxborough left the world of sports to attend the University of Detroit Law School and to become the first black State Senator in Michigan.

John Roxborough met Joe Louis at Brewster where Joe won 50 of his 54 amateur fights. Roxborough, impressed by Joe's boxing skills, became Joe's manager when he turned professional in 1933 after winning the Golden Gloves championship. Joe Louis was strong and tough when he and Roxborough met, but Joe was rough-hewn. John Roxborough fine-tuned Joe, grooming him for his role as Heavyweight

Champion of the World. John is credited for developing Joe's boxing career.

Leon "Toy" Wheeler, Coach Extraordinaire

In 1969, the center known since 1929 as Brewster Center was renamed the Wheeler Recreation Center in honor of Leon "Toy" Wheeler. The center, located at 637 Brewster, has been a landmark sports and cultural facility for the black community since its inception. As Brewster Center, no one was more essential to the successful athletic programs that endured for many years than Leon Wheeler. Wheeler was the alpha and the omega of Brewster Center. He was the man who ran the center and established programs in swimming, tennis, basketball and boxing. Wheeler organized the boxing program that produced many great fighters that include Joe Louis, Jimmy Edgar, Ray Barnes, Sugar Ray Robinson and a host of others. Wheeler was a pioneer for African-American athletes and for inner city youth. In 1919, he became

Leon "Toy" Wheeler

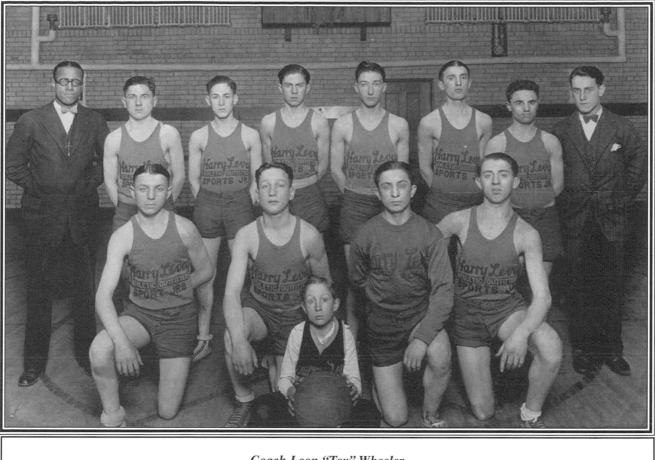

Coach Leon "Toy" Wheeler

the first black recreation worker employed by the City of Detroit. Wheeler was no stranger to sports and to sportsmanlike conduct. In high school, Wheeler received four sports awards and went on to become an outstanding college athlete. In 1978 Leon was inducted into Wayne State University Athletic Hall of Fame for his outstanding prowess in football, basketball and track.

ERNEST WAGNER, OUTSTANDING ATHLETE

Ernest Wagner's interest in competitive sports became evident at an early age. Gus Finney, an Ex Harlem Globetrotter, then a recreation instructor at the Balch School playground, was the catalyst. Finney introduced Wagner to baseball and basketball, sports that were to play an important part in his adult life.

When Wagner entered Northeastern High School in 1947, he played basketball and baseball. In his senior year, Wagner garnered an Eastside championship in baseball and basketball. He was selected to the All City and to the All State basketball teams Wagner was recruited by the University of Michigan the first year that the school recruited African-American basketball players. He ended up accepting a scholarship to Wayne State University. While at Wayne State, he became one-fifth of the unit that gave the school the title, " the first college team in Michigan to play five African-Americans" or what Dr. John Kline called, "Five Black Players on the Floor." The Associated Press rated this team 18th in the nation in the 1951-1952 season. The 1952-1953 pre- season poll rated the team that included Charlie Primus, John Kline, Paul Dean, Robert Boyce and Wally Ziemba in the top ten. John Kline was picked pre- season All-American.

Recruited by the Milwaukee Hawks and the Harlem Globetrotters, in 1954, Wagner dropped

149

out of college, tried out with both teams, but made the decision to play with the Harlem Globetrotters from 1954-1967. Wagner still resides in Detroit with his wife, Denise Hall Wagner and works with "The Legends of Black Basketball."

Gus Finney, Detroit Legend

John Kline has described Gus Finney as being a great coach and a great human being. Kline says, "If a role model can illustrate by example, I can't think of a better person. He represented character, sportsmanship…he tried to help every person he came in contact with." Gus attended Miller High School where he ran track, played baseball and helped win a city championship in soccer while attending Miller. Basketball, however, was the sport in which he distinguished himself. Finney competed for two years as a Harlem Globetrotter during their lean years, when the take on some nights was only ten dollars.

Finney was truly exceptional as a coach and a role model. He was employed by Parks and Recreation to work five days a week, but he donated his Sundays to the Sunday League, which he administered. This league was known throughout the Midwest as the best. The teams Finney coached won eleven championships in 14 years during the 1941-53 period.

Finney mentored and coached all of the guys who went on to become Globetrotters: Murphy Summers, Sammy Gee, Ernest Wagner, Charles Henry, David Gaines and John Kline. It was Finney's skill at coaching these guys, their ability to play basketball and Finney's recommendation that guided them to become Globetrotters.

Harlem Globetrotters Front-liners (L to R) Bobby Milton, Herman Taylor & Ernie Wagner.

Larry Bleach, a University of Detroit "First."

Gus Finney

Larry Bleach, 1st Black Basketball Player for University of Detroit.

Larry Bleach made history by being the first African-American player at the University of Detroit in 1932. John Kline recalls an interview with Bleach in 1980 in which Bleach reflects on his first road trip with the team. "The first trip I took with the team to play Loyola University in Chicago, the other team members were lodged in separate rooms at the hotel. The bellboy knocked on the door and said, 'Mr. Bleach, I'll show you an exit convenient for you to use.' It was the fire escape."

Because of his superior ability, Bleach eventually became captain of the team. After an outstanding college career, Bleach distinguished himself as a basketball player with the Globetrotters, the Great Lakes Big Five and the Detroit Brown Bombers. Bleach was among the first black players inducted into the Professional Basketball Hall of Fame.

When his basketball career ended, Bleach distinguished himself as a policeman for 25 years, earning 16 citations and becoming one of the first black detectives in the city. Joining Stroh's Brewery in 1962, Bleach became Stroh's Brewery's first director of community relations in 1970.

John Henry
Chicago Cubs 3rd Baseman

In The Bleachers at Briggs Stadium,
A group of football fans enjoying the game (circa 1930's).

Mayor Coleman Young with the Brewster "Old Timers." Photo includes Erma Henderson, former City Council woman, Judge Jessie Slayton, Emanuel Stewart, and former City Clerk, Jim Bradley.

1949 Postal Alliance Bowling League

Forest Club Monthly

FREE COPY ★ ★ ★ ★ No. 2 ★ ★ ★ ★ JUNE 1945

Edited and Published Under Supervision of the . . . . Regent Figure Skating Club

Forest Club Skaters Sweep Nationals At Cleveland, Ohio

Woodchoppers Win Forest Club Leagues Championship

In a spectacular finish the Forest Club League wound up the season Monday evening, May 28th, with Harding's Woodchoppers finishing in the number one position.

With the Forest Club Roller Rink team, who finished second, it was a nip-and-tuck race all through the season for the Woodchoppers, with both teams ending with a team average tie of 808.

The third position goes to the Wolves, who were really laying in the pocket at the finish, and had the season lasted a few more weeks might have finished a notch or two higher with the help of their star ace, McKinley Woody, who was shooting in the 2's almost at will.

The championship Woodchoppers team lineup consisted of Virginia Sauls, Joe King, Eddie Richmond, A. Scott and R. Van Buren.

Honorable mention goes to the following Forest Club League bowlers who are really worth watching: George Green, Claude McKee, Connie Ware, Eddie Richmond, Johnnie Johnson and McKinley Woody. Big time talent scouts take notice.

Looking at the funny side, might I say that the season's Ham prize should go to the league's loudest bowler, Mr. Charles Thomas, who shot a big 69 one evening, rolling 10 complete frames without a mark.

Wm. Lane, manager of the Forest Club alleys, announces the opening of summer leagues around June 15th, with the following events scheduled: Ladies' Night every Monday, with special rates of 25c per game. Couples' night every Tuesday, 25c per game; Junior league 5-man teams for boys aged 16 down, every Saturday afternoon, 1 to 5 p. m. at 20c per game, and 5-man teams' league night at 25c per game. If you are interested in joining any of these leagues, apply at the desk immediately.

Mr. Lane also announced that the new summer bowling alley hours are as follows: Week days, 6 p. m. to 2 a. m.; Saturdays,

Kathlene Moore Takes Ladies National Singles Skating Title

Detroit's own Forest Club skaters upset all the expert predictions by taking the big end of the majority of championship events at Cleveland last month.

Skating with the ease and grace of a seasoned veteran, Kathleene Moore of the Forest Club was crowned Queen of the ladies singles free style event, with Dorothy Saunder of Cleveland finishing a close second and June Alexander, also of Cleveland, finishing third.

In the men's free style singles, Roy Harris of Cleveland finished in the first position with Nick Ball of Chicago taking second place and Nimrod Bowman of Cleveland finishing third.

James Stone and Jessie Canty of Detroit won first place in the free style pairs event, with James Berry and Alice Morrow of Detroit taking second, and Clarence Anderson of Flint, coupling with Minnie Battle of Detroit finishing third.

For the Collegiate, only three couples entered, with none from Detroit, and only one prize was awarded, that going to Dorothy Saunders and Nimrod Bowman of Cleveland.

In the fourteen-step competition only a few couples entered this also, and Dorothy Saunders and Nimrod Bowman were again the winners.

For the Circle Waltz championship the entry was very large, with couples from five cities taking part. The judges only awarded one prize, with this going to Alice Morrow and James Berry of Detroit.

In the speed skating events the thrills

Super Market Planned For Forest Club

One of Detroit's finest Super Markets is now being planned by Mr. Bunnie Wilson to be located in the Forest Club Annex.

Architectural drawings already completed show that this market will be one of the most beautiful and finest Super Markets in Detroit and operated exclusively by Negroes.

Opening dates have not been announced yet, but Mr. Wilson informs me that when this market is opened it will be equal or superior to any market in the city of Detroit and far

and spills were plentiful, with the sideline handicappers offering all kinds of odds, and taking anything from a nickle to a twenty.

Twenty starters took off in the men's senior 440-yard speed race, but only three or four were able to finish, with first place going to Paul White of Cleveland, and Nick Ball, the Chicago speedster, finishing second.

In the boys' junior 440-yard race, Nimrod Bowman finished first and Roy Harris finished second, both being Cleveland boys. Calvin Taylor, Detroit's hope, couldn't stand the grind and fell by the wayside.

The 880-yard race was much too long a grind for most of the large field of starters. This race was 28 laps but by the

continued on page 3

SUMMER SKATING SCHEDULE

Beginning, Wednesday, June 13th

EVERY WEDNESDAY
8:30 to 11:30 P.M.

154

Gray-Swift Basketball Team, Bethel A.M.E. Church (1926).

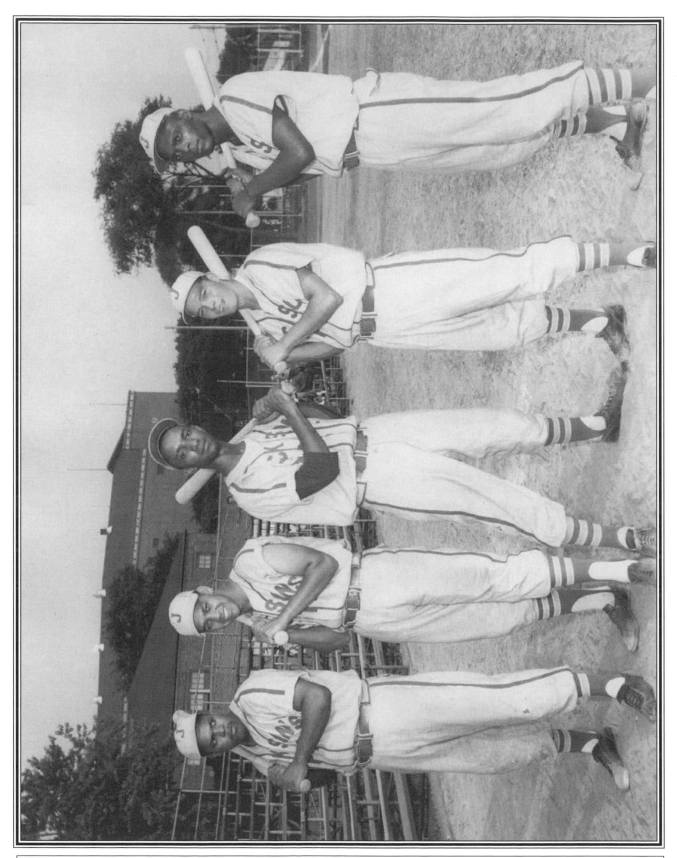

Jackson Apartments Class A / Detroit Amateur Baseball Federation
Players L to R - Unknown, John Henry, John Cunningham, Walter Banks & Charles Duncan.

CHAPTER TEN
OUR CULTURAL CENTERS
COUNTING OUR BLESSINGS

Whenever we Near East Siders count our blessings, we give thanks for having had the good fortune to grow up in an area that embraced the cultural center of Detroit, and through this cultural Mecca, embraced those of us who were lucky enough to live on the Near Eastside. It is no exaggeration to say that the Near Eastside was the heart of the cultural scene for black Detroiters. The Main Public Library, the Detroit Institute of Arts, the historic churches, the fraternity houses, the fraternal orders, the YWCA, the Urban League, the Brewster Center, the skating rinks, dance halls, movie theaters, and yes, the nightclubs and bars, all reposed within the boundaries of the Near Eastside.

We are reminded that all blessings come with a cost. Ours? Many, perhaps most of us, were so content, so mesmerized with the plethora of arts and entertainment, the culture, the fun available on the Near Eastside of Detroit, that there was an unwillingness or perhaps a disinterest in seeking the larger world of Detroit that existed outside our defined boundaries. Many were too comfortable seeing the world come to the Near Eastside to venture out to what has become known as Metro Detroit. And *the world* did come! The West Siders, the *Elites* from the North End, the

Conant Garden residents and those from the Far Eastside of Detroit, all came to the Near Eastside because the Near Eastside was the lifeblood of black Detroit. This was where life *happened*.

The Near Eastside was not only alive; it was *live* in all of its blackness and relative poverty. The consequence? Most Detroiters knew the Near Eastside of Detroit, used it, reveled in it and in a curious way, reviled and maligned it. On the other hand, many Near East Siders had a somewhat myopic view of what life was like in Metro Detroit. All knew Belle Isle, many knew Eastwood Park and downtown Detroit with its J.L.Hudson building, but many others knew little else except vicariously. The savvier or perhaps the more adventurous Near Eastsiders visited the popular party scene that was a constant at the Nacairema Club on the West Side. Others frequented the West End Hotel in Southwest Detroit to listen to the fine jazz played there on weekends. Even fewer visited the "Sweet Eater," a popular soda fountain type hangout for teens in Conant Gardens. One might say that the little bit of cultural heaven available on the Near Eastside was so attractive, so addictive, that many saw no reason to venture outside.

Lucy Thurman YWCA

157

Eating and drinking have always been a part of the culture of people, and nowhere was this truer than on the Near Eastside of Detroit. Many of us had our first experiences in fine dining at the Gotham Hotel Dining Room or the elegant Blue Room at the Lucy Thurman YWCA. We learned about Jewish cuisine while dining at Samuel's restaurant in the Eastern Market. Some of us had our first introduction to food traditionally Mexican by purchasing *hot tamales* from a stand on Canfield and Beaubien outside of the Parrot Bar. Our introduction to Chinese food may have come from our experiences dining at Stanley's Mania on Canfield or the China Casino on John R. Street. Our budding familiarity with the foods of mainstream America and outside of the traditional black or "soul" foods encouraged many of us to experiment with cultures other than our own.

There were many movie houses on the Near Eastside of Detroit. Before the advent of television and while integration was still a dream, movies were one of the main forms of entertainment for youths and adults. But movies were not just entertainment. Movies were our first Social Studies class as they allowed viewers to enter a world to which they were strangers. We learned about the desert southwest from the old oaters, about Transylvania and its environs from the Count Dracula movies. Even from the sometimes deliberately misleading presentations that reinforced the old racial stereotypes, we learned something of what life might be like in China, Hawaii or Africa. The weekly newsreels, "The Eyes and Ears of the World," taught us some of the horrors and realities of wartime life in Europe and Asia.

In 1927, the Detroit YWCA established the **Lucy Thurman YWCA** for "colored" girls and women. It was named for a pioneering women's temperance leader, Lucy Thurman. In 1928, the Detroit YWCA established Camp Norcom in Dexter, Michigan for "Negro" girls. The Lucy Thurman Y was located on Elizabeth and St. Antoine Street on the Near Eastside. Because of local ordinances, the Lucy Thurman Y had to be segregated from the Caucasian branch, which was located around the corner. The residents were primarily young women who came to Detroit from the South to find employment.

The Lucy Thurman Y played an integral role in the black community. Famous entertainers and the social elite had many special social and cultural events at the Lucy Thurman. Recitals, teas, engagement parties, wedding showers and bridge parties were often held at the Lucy Thurman. There was an elegant "Blue Room" that had a reputation for elegance. The "Blue Room" was one place where black Detroiters went when they wanted meals prepared to perfection. The "Blue Room" was famous for its crabmeat salad, rolls and sweet potato pies created by Frances L. Owens, who served as Food Service Director for more than a decade and later became Director of Food Service at the Gotham Hotel. There was also a cafeteria where members and residents dined and where the food was also prepared to perfection.

For many teenagers, the Lucy Thurman was a haven, a safe place to go and have fun, to mix and mingle with the boys, chaperoned, of course. On weekends, there were often dances with live, young local talent supplying the entertainment. Guitarist, Kenny Burrell was one of the young Detroit musicians who entertained at these dances, and who wowed the teenagers with his striking good looks. The Lucy Thurman Y also hosted pajama parties for the Y Teens on some weekend or summer nights. It was not just a place; the Lucy Thurman was a *destination.* **Sylvia Braithwaite Muthleb,** a Near Eastsider, remembers the Lucy Thurman YWCA as the place where she spent many Saturdays swimming, dancing, roller-skating, socializing and playing ping-pong. Another Near Eastsider **Era Irving Williamson,** remembers fondly, the Summer Home Camp at the Lucy Thurman where she and others would go every weekday, take their lunches, participate in a variety of joyful experiences, return home invigorated at the end of the day, then revisit the next day.

————

The St. Antoine YMCA at the corner of Elizabeth and St. Antoine was an important center for Detroit's black community. It had the best recreational facilities and staff for its youth, but it was also a meeting place for business, civic and social organizations. On Sundays, its large gym hosted forums and lectures by many national political and civic leaders. It was important to black youths in all parts of the city because there was segregation at other YMCA and YWCA branches. Even if you lived

(Above) The Detroit Institute of Arts.　　(Below) The Detroit Public Library.

Detroit Conservatory of Music, Woodward Avenue.

Urban League, Mack & John R..

Detroit Association of Women's Club, Brush & Ferry.

Center Theatre, Woodward & E. Grand Blvd, 1936.

St. Antoine YMCA Site

Your Heritage Museum for Children

across from the Fisher Branch YMCA, you were not allowed to use their facilities.

Imagine living in an area where much of the collected knowledge of the known world could be found? This was the **Detroit's Main Public Library** on the west side of Woodward at Kirby Street. This was the one place every neighborhood child frequented, some rarely, some weekly and some almost daily. This is where children could go to hear someone read the exciting fairy tales and interesting stories of other children in other lands Many of the younger children visiting the children's room were anxiously awaiting the day they would be old enough to get an *adult* library card and get an opportunity to read the *real* books. In those years, one could borrow to take home, books from the Rare Book Collection. From these library experiences, we learned library etiquette and a respect for books. One Near Eastsider recalls going to the Main Public Library with friends, checking out as many books as allowed, then taking the books and sitting on the Art Institute Lawn to read and to pick crab apples.

The Detroit Institute of Arts was one of the Near Eastside's greatest assets. It had just about everything that children and adults found interesting, exciting or fun. Surrounded by beautiful and spacious grounds, the Art Institute, as it was popularly called, attracted young and old alike. For those with political interests, there was the famous mural, Detroit Industry, painted by Diego Rivera that depicted Detroit's factory workers as chattels of the auto Industry.. For those with more prurient interests, there was "The Wedding Dance" by Pieter Breugels that would have shown graphic representations of male genitalia had they not been covered by codpieces. Viewing the skeleton or the several mummies that the museum housed in its Egyptian wing could probably satisfy any interests in the macabre. All of the famous *masters* could be found here, Rembrandt, El Greco, Rodin, Vincent van Gogh, and Picasso to name a few. Classes in painting, sculpture and pottery making were held at the museum. For a number of years, there was a Unity or All Souls Church that held services in the auditorium on Sundays.

The Detroit Urban League dates back to 1916 when Forrester B. Washington served as the first executive director and Henry G. Stevens as president.

It was located on the southeast corner of Erskinc and John R. Today it is the site of a Michigan Historical Marker that was registered in 1979. The Urban League's initial purpose was the improvement of the social, moral, and material status of the large numbers of blacks who migrated to Detroit during the 1920's and beyond. This included seeking housing and employment opportunities for blacks. Under John Dancy, executive director from 1918-1960, the Urban League expanded its mission to include a variety of social services that included health care and recreational facilities. Later, the Urban League moved to its present site at Mack and John R.

The Detroit Urban League was not just about jobs and housing. It was about teaching black people to live well, if not grandly. It offered as a part of its program, facilities for weddings, receptions, teas and other civic affairs. While the Detroit Urban League had a strict policy of no alcoholic beverages being served at any affair in their building, it was very popular with Detroit society, society with a capital S and with a small s. On one of the walls of the Detroit Urban League was a painting of a large eye that seemed to follow wherever one walked in the building. The intent of the artist is not known, but it was a constant reminder that one is always being observed and that one should temper his or her behavior accordingly.

Where the neighborhood and the families were sometimes lacking in cultural inspiration, the Near Eastside churches stepped up to the plate. As a case in point, **Bethel A.M.E.** had a **"Housewives League"** organized by Mrs. Fannie B. Peck, wife of the then current minister. There was also a **"Junior Housewives League"** that met every week at a neighbor's home, a Mrs. Ashford. Teola Cranon Hunter was its first president. At these meetings, adult and young adult women were taught about black history, culture and etiquette by the more "culturally experienced" adults. Here we were taught how to set a proper table and the correct way to prepare and pour tea. We were taught the importance of speaking correct English. There was an emphasis at these meetings was on how to dress properly and to be a proper lady at all times.

One group of protestant churches organized a city wide "Older Boys and Girls" Conference that brought youth together for meetings and lectures at the St.

161

Antoine Y and the Lucy Thurman Y. At the Near Eastside's **Second Baptist Church** during the Depression Years, the Richard B. Harrison Players of Detroit staged many plays and musicals in Michigan and in Canada under the leadership of Mrs. Jerome Macklin. Their early productions included "The Little Foxes" and "Murder in the Cathedral." Later productions included "The Robe" and "The People vs. Pontius Pilate."

The Detroit Conservatory of Music is located on Woodward Avenue just south of what used to be The Maccabees Building and is now The School Centers Building. The Detroit Conservatory was *the place* aspiring black musician wanted to attend in the years 1940-1960 if they wanted classical training in music. The lessons were more expensive than the black music studios charged, but certainly a bit more prestigious. None of the instructors at the conservatory were black at that time as the preeminence of black musicianship had yet to be acknowledged. One of our Near Eastsiders, Eugene Elzy, and many other Detroit musicians of note attended this conservatory. These musicians used the classical training received at the conservatory as a stepping-stone to learning and perfecting the music of the times.

The existence of three major black college fraternities in Detroit might well remind one of the axiom, "The whole is worth more than the sum of its parts." The impact of the **Alpha Phi Alpha**, the **Kappa Alpha Psi** and the **Omega Psi Phi** fraternities in Detroit's Near Eastside cannot be overestimated. The presence of these fraternities added deeply and significantly to Detroit's black landscape. These fraternities were a focal point for black social, cultural, educational and community service activities in an era when there were few other outlets.

The fraternity houses were all located on the Near Eastside of Detroit, the Alpha House (Gamma Lambda Chapter) at 293 Eliot Street, the Kappa House (Detroit Alumni Chapter) at 269 Erskine and the Omega House (Nu Omega Chapter) at 235 East Ferry Street. The Gamma Lambda Chapter of the Alphas was the first. It was organized in 1919 in the offices of physicians M.E. Morton and J. Gregory. at 1721 St. Antoine Street. The Alphas have been at their present quarters since May 15, 1939. The Detroit Alumni Chapter of the Kappa Alpha Psi fraternity was founded on April 3,

1920 by brothers who were alumni of Delta Chapter at Wilberforce University in Ohio. The Kappa's permanent house was not purchased until September 7, 1944. The Nu Omega Chapter of the Omegas was chartered in 1923 with 26 chapter members. The Omega House at 235 East Ferry was acquired in the early 1940's. The building had been a YMCA boarding home for boys.

Whereas the private goals and aims of the fraternities were equally lofty, it was said that the public persona of the fraternities was different. If one thinks of these three fraternities in Freudian terms, the Omegas would be the *Id*; the Kappas would be the *Ego* and the Alphas, the *Superego*. The Omega men were considered the fun lovers, the adventurous, and the athletes. The Kappa men were considered egotistical and arrogant and more often than not, handsome The Alpha men were generally thought of as brainy but serious and somewhat staid and conventional in their beliefs and their behavior.

The Omega House was the fraternity house where young people went to drink, to dance and to party in a spirited way. It was a cheerful and somewhat laid-back house with a basement bar and juke box. Decorous behavior was not strictly demanded nor enforced. It was not unusual for strong public disagreements to occur at the Omega House at a weekend affair. The music may have often been canned, but the dancing was *live*. An extra-added attraction to the Omega House was its proximity to the Crafts Men's Club at 275 E. Ferry, a large house that was practically an adjunct to the Omega House. This is where those who wanted to dance to live music went when they left the Omega House.

The Kappa House on Erskine tended to be more conventional in the affairs they sponsored, a little more formal and with a tad more elegance. The behaviors at the Kappa House were more controlled, decorum more often in the forefront. Appearances mattered! The fraternity was rife with handsome men, the egos of which were legendary. Many behaved as if they believed what their song says, "You must be a Kappa Alpha Psi if you want to go to heaven when you die." The Kappas hosted many great parties. You were not a part of the "in crowd" if you had not been invited to the Kappa House.

Omega Fraternity House on Ferry.

Kappa Fraternity House on Erskine.

163

Alpha Fraternity House on Eliot.

It is difficult to describe the **Alpha House** for very few non-Alphas ever entered it. The Alphas themselves were inclined to party at other fraternity houses. It was said that the Alpha House had a housemother who was in charge of the perceived moral standards of the Alpha men and their role in the community. This attitude put a serious damper on the possibility of a party atmosphere. Convivial and hospitable or not, the Alpha men were and continue to be respected for their perceived superior intellect, their attention to business, thus their economic potential. Alpha men were the kind of men the more judicious and pragmatic young women wanted to marry.

Today, these three fraternity houses still stand in their long time locations on the Near Eastside of Detroit. They are continuing their legacy of community service activities. Over the years, each fraternity has donated generously to the Negro College Fund and granted many scholarship awards to deserving students. The Alpha House has been designated as a Historic Site by the State of Michigan. The Omega House is located in an area that has been named "The Talented Tenth District."

There were other organizations that were culturally relevant to African-Americans in Detroit.

Perhaps foremost among these is the **NAACP**. The NAACP had several chapters, one of which was in the Brewster Housing Project. The youth groups in this chapter and others were active both politically and socially. The **NAACP** sponsored dances, conferences and other activities important to young people. Commonly, there would be plans for combating discrimination in hiring practices in restaurants and in other public facilities that discriminated against blacks. Sometimes a group of teens teamed up with a Caucasian group at a house on Boston Boulevard called CO-OP House. At CO-OP house, there was singing of songs such as "The More We Get Together, The Happier We Will Be." Country dancing was also a part of the meetings that included brainstorming for ways to combat racism and frequent talk of world peace. These mixed-race meetings were relatively rare in the culture during the forties and were important as a way of teens meeting teens unlike themselves.

We are fortunate that in this city where urban renewal has often meant urban removal, many of the cultural icons, the buildings described in this chapter, still exist and are available for our use.

———

Amity Social Club Fashion Show, El Sino Club / (L to R) Terry Bagwell, Ruth Dick, Lena Taylor, Betty Hall, Delores Trotter, Mildred Barksdale, & Alice Smith.

Louise Williams and some Near Eastsiders Party at The Alpha House.

John Cozart

Louise Williams

Bob Thomas

The Original Ten Gentlemen. Pictured are Sylvester Jenkins, John Burrell, (Treasurer), John Royster, J.D. Douglas (President), Robert Perry, Forrest Strickland, George Montgomery and Alvin Reid. Not pictured are Donald Stark, William Smith and Joel Kline.

Kappa Pledgees: (Rear L to R) Karl Farrah, Winston Lang, Parker Wortham, Melvin Hollowell, Leon Wingo, James Leigh, Donald Godbold, Craig, John Hazley, Ralph Patterson, Kenneth Walker.
(Front L to R) Herman Blackshear, Lawrence Jackson, George Gaines, unknown, and Jessie Odum..
(Not pictured is the photographer, Joynal A. Muthleb, the 18th pledgee.)

Kappa's Black and White (1956). Among those pictured are: Robert Boyce, Betty Williams, Eugene McGuire, Garland Jaggers, Charles McIntosh, John Cox, George Duncan, Carol Granberry, Charles Boyce, Glenda Boyce, John Burrell and Mattie Burrell.

167

Omega Court: Teola Cranon, Gloria ?, Barbara Giles, Doris Palmer and Doris Smart (front).

Joe Kelly, Calvin Taylor, Freda Rentie & Alvin Cain at The Forest Club Roller Rink, 1949.

Council Cargle stars in The Detroit Civic Players' "Home of The Brave," 1955.

A Christmas Concert at Northeastern High School.

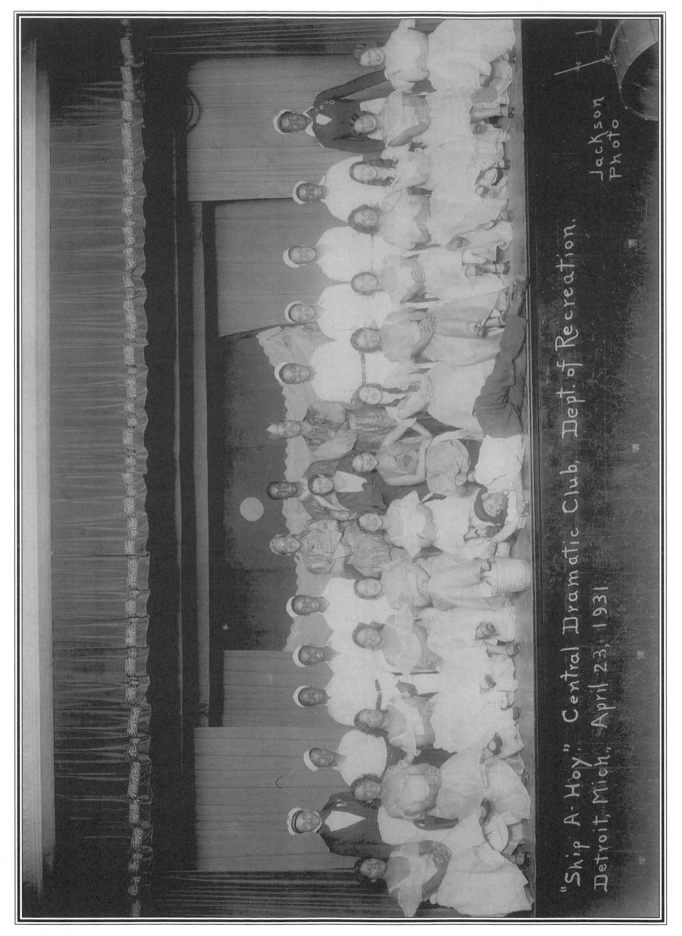

"Ship-A-Hoy", Central Dramatic Club, Dept. of Recreation, Detroit, Mich., April 23, 1931.

Jackson Photo

170

Elizabeth Palmer & Harry Quarles Wedding, 1940.

Duane Johnson w/Alice Hodo, Irene Bearden, Jimmy Palms, Justine Rogers w/Eugene Cunningham, Yvonne Rogers w/Victor Majors and Ralph Walton, 1949.

East Ferry: Avenue of Dreams

Detroit's 300th Birthday

Middle-class blacks create an oasis

Activists establish schools, hospitals and cultural centers

Courtesy of Phyllis Lewis Ponders

Violet Lewis, center, introduced her daughter, Phyllis, left, to Detroit's African American society and welcomed her daughter, Marjorie, right, home from college, with a June garden party in 1945. It was an event that stopped traffic outside the Lewis College of Business.

The Peck Teens
request the honor of your
presence at their
Sweethearts Rose Semi-formal
Wednesday February 14, 1951
seven o'clock p.m.
William H. Peck Center
Detroit, Michigan

("BEAUTY IS TRUTH, TRUTH BEAUTY"
KEATS

DEPARTMENT OF PARKS & RECREATION
DETROIT

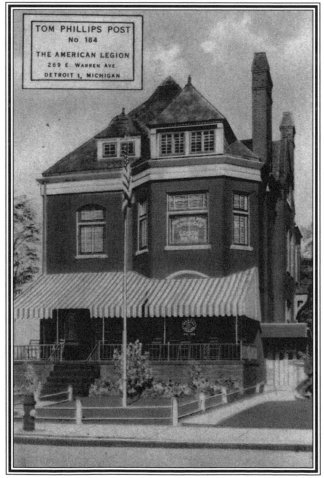

TOM PHILLIPS POST
No 184
THE AMERICAN LEGION
269 E. WARREN AVE.
DETROIT 1, MICHIGAN

172

Jackie Spencer and Vivian Bonds dancing the "Jitterbug" in rear of the Detroit Institute of Arts.

Clarence Brown in front of the DIA.

Brother Kappa Ushers at Wedding of Conrad Mallet to Gwendolyn Jones.
(L to R) Joynal Muthleb, Julius Coombs, unknown, Benjamin Druitt, Roland Dean, and Charles Smith.

173

Howard Givens and Eloise Terrian Porter's wedding party. April 15, 1953.

Yvonne Rogers Bridal Shower, June 19, 1950. (Standing, L to R): Unk, Irene Pettiford, Jewell Smith. Unk.
(Seated, L to R): Betty Stewart, Alice Hodo, Yvonne Rogers, Marian Hunter and Barbara Lewis.

(L to R) Jessie Bogwell, Biddie and Louise Gibson
Biddie and Jessie Faithful owned a restaurant on St. Antoine.

Julia Lee Carter and Willie Raines' Reception.

Past Presidents of the Housewives' League

CHRISTINE FUQUA
1939 - 1945

GERTRUDE J. ROGERS
1945-1946

NANNIE E. BLACK
1946-1952 (Deceased)

HELEN MALLOY
1952 - 1956

MRS. FANNIE B. PECK
Founder
1930 - 1939

LUCILLE JONES
1956 - 1960

NAOMI JEFFRIES
1960 - 1964

CAMILLA HOLDEN
1964 - 1968

MARIE DESSAW
1968 - 1971

Albert & Mamie Cheatham's home, 655 E. Kirby. A birthday celebration honoring Fannie B. Peck (seated on sofa). Guests include Allison Cargle, Eddye Rowlette, Council Cargle, Ruperta Fleming, Veronica Webster, Aleta Webster, Dianne Elzy, Helen Praither, Alice Cargle and Albert Townes.

Doris Carter and friends celebrating at the Craftsman Club on East Ferry.

Edmonson Wedding Bells

Florence and Arthur

Lois Ruth and Clarence

Charles and Elisabeth

William and Betty

Chapter Eleven
The Near Eastsiders Group:
Some Biographical Notes

We are the **Near Eastsiders.** We have been nurtured by the vitality of our schools, our churches, and our remarkable cultural center. We come from the part of Detroit that Berry Gordy, of Motown fame, when describing his family's move from the Westside to the Eastside in his autobiography, *To Be Loved*, writes; "It was like moving from the country to the city. There were so many different kinds of people, most of them were smart, hip people who wanted to be somebody." We are *those* people. Gordy says further, "The Near Eastside kids are just hipper, sharper an funnier." We are *those* people too.

We are the people who danced in the streets when our own hero, Joe Louis Barrow won his fights. We are the people who bore the brunt of the 1943 riots yet emerged from that trauma to build better and stronger neighborhoods. We are the people who have witnessed Hastings Street at night when it was lit up like a Christmas tree, even though some of us were not allowed to venture on it. We are *those* people. We are the **Near Eastsiders.** Come read about us.

Joynal A. Muthleb

Detroit Police Officer from 1956-1960. Resigned from the Police Department in 1960 to pursue a career with the Detroit Board of Education as a Certified Special Education Teacher. Retired after thirty years service with the Detroit Board of Education in 1986.

Joynal A. Muthleb was the fourth child born to parents, Abdul and Huldah Muthleb. His siblings were brothers Abdul and Ahmed and Sisters Mildred and Zebadah. The family lived on Alexanderine, Rivard and Forest on Detroit's Eastside. Joynal attended Lincoln and Trowbridge Elementary School, Garfield Intermediate School, Cass Technical High School and Wayne University. From 1944 to 1945 served in the United States Army as a Corporal in Austria and Germany. After an honorable discharge from the Armed Services, attended Wayne University earning a Bachelors and a Masters Degree in Special Education. He was a

William Wesley Edmonson, Sr. is the seventh of eight children born to John Henry and Georgia Edmonson. The family lived at 414 Hendrie with their dog, Mickey. All of the family were members of Bethel A.M.E Church. Active at Bethel, he was a member of the Youth Choir and in addition, was in Boy Scout Troop 166. Edmonson clerked at Schmit Drugstore on Palmer and Brush Street and delivered the Detroit Times and Michigan Chronicle newspapers in the neighborhood. Additionally, he set type and ran the press for Sanders Printing Company. He attended Balch Elementary, Garfield Intermediate, Northeastern

Torrance Alvin Cain

William Edmonson, III

High School and Wayne State University. Edmonson served in the Korean War, worked for D.S.R., Parks & Recreation, Traffic Engineering, and retired from Michigan Bell Telephone. He remembers Hastings Street which was a major business thoroughfare housing restaurants, bars, theaters, clothing stores and shoe shops. Says Edmonson, "There were always people on the street. I could travel day or night and was never afraid. The adults were nurturing and protective of their children and seniors. There was always a helping hand to anyone in need. This was a great neighborhood to live in."

Torrance Alvin Cain, a native Detroiter, lived with his parents Maud and Earl Cain on Medbury between Hastings and Rivard. He attended Balch Elementary School, Garfield and McMichael Intermediate Schools, Northern High School and Wayne State University's College of Liberal Arts...Cain served 16 months in Korea during the Korean War then worked as a Design Draftsman and enrolled in Engineering at The Detroit Institute of Technology. In 1960 Cain began working for The Bendix Corporation in Southfield, MI, subsequently enrolling in Lawrence Institute of Technology and graduating with a Bachelor of Science Degree in Mechanical Engineering. Cain says," During my 50 years working in the Engineering Field, one of my most notable tasks was working for a subcontractor of NASA (The Bendix Corporation)

Council Cargle

Lenore Lewis Lawson Evans

Florence Rowlette Lawson

Sylvia Braithwaite Muthleb

on the Apollo Man Space Landing on the Moon." Subsequently, Cain worked for General Motors at the GM Technology Center in Warren, MI. retiring in 2001.

Council Cargle is a homegrown talent, born and raised on the Near Eastside of Detroit on East Kirby. He lived there until he was twenty-one years old. What we now know as "The Cultural Center" was his playground. He attended Balch Elementary School, Garfield Intermediate and Northeastern High School. The Detroit Institute of Arts, the Main Public Library, and the Children's Museum were all within walking distance and were instrumental in his development as an actor. Council was acting from the age of eight, putting on performances in neighbor's garages or in his basement and charging the audience ten cents. At Northeastern, he became President of the Drama Club. He studied acting at Wayne State University.

Lenore Lewis Lawson Evans is one of seven children born to George and Mattie Lewis. Lenore lived on Hendrie Street near Hastings and attended Balch Elementary, Garfield Intermediate, Cass Technical High School and Wayne State University. She graduated from M.D.T.A. School of Nursing. Lenore has worked as an elevator operator, a Telephone Girl for Michigan Bell, for Jacobson's and Winkelmans as a manager. As a nurse, she worked at Grace and Sinai Hospital. For many years Lenore worked as a licensed travel agent, sharing her passion for travel with friends and clients. Lenore attends All Saints Church where she has been a member since 1969.

Florence Rowlette Lawson was born in Kentucky and moved to Detroit in 1943 where she lived with her parents, Charles and Eddye Rowlette and siblings Ilma and Coranell Rowlette on 436 Hendrie. Florence was a member of Bethel A.M. E. Church on Frederick and St. Antoine. She attended Balch Elementary, Garfield Intermediate and Northwestern High School. She also attended Michigan State Normal (now Eastern Michigan University) and Wayne State University. She was employed with the Bell System, Michigan Bell and the New York Telephone Company. Florence moved to New York in 1964. Since the death of her husband, she now divides her time between New York and Detroit. This transition is made easier because of many fond memories and especially of family and the friendships that still remain.

Sylvia (Braithwaite) Muthleb was born in Detroit to Cecil and Olga Braithwaite, West Indian immigrants from Trinidad, British West Indies. Sylvia lived with her parents and siblings, Cynthia, John and Cyril at 636 Hendrie where her father was caretaker of a 12-unit apartment building. Later the parents bought their first home at 662 Harper. She attended Balch Elementary, Sherrard Intermediate, and Cass Technical High School and graduated from Holy Rosary High School. Sylvia attended Wayne University for 2 ½ years before beginning work for American Telegraph & Telephone as a Long Distance Operator, later joining Michigan Bell Telephone for a career that spanned 33 years.

———

Erma Harris Zachary

Erma Harris Zachary is the only child born to Willie Ermie Harris and Clinton Walter Harris. She first lived with her parents on Palmer between St. Antoine and Beaubien. Later the family moved to Medbury Street near Brush, and finally to 604 Hendrie near the corner of St. Antoine.

Erma attended the Balch Elementary School where she learned to swim in the second grade. Among herd fondest memories are taking walks with her mother across the school playground then walking a few blocks more to the Warfield Theater. Erma remembers, also, the sounds and smells of the local vendors as saloons, fish markets and drugstores and pawnshops.

Other memories are lunching at the Gotham Hotel and enjoying the great live musical shows at the Paradise Theatre. Erma moved from the Near Eastside when she was twelve years old and completed her education at Custer Elementary School, Sherrard Intermediate and Cass Technical High School. After graduating High School, Erma worked in the personnel department of Michigan Bell Telephone Company.

———

Dorothy Greenfield Hill

Dorothy Greenfield Hill lived with her family, parents Naomi and Alfred Hill and brothers, Alfred

John A. Henry

Robert L. Ellison

but also the home of the Greenfield family's business, the **Eagle Moving Company**. Dorothy attended Trowbridge School, Garfield Intermediate and Northeastern   Dorothy attended Plymouth Congregational Church where she taught Sunday school classes. She worked in Wayne State Cafeteria to augment her income on her way to earning a B.A. in Education plus 30 hours as an Education Specialist at Wayne State University.

Dorothy began her teaching career as a substitute teacher at Trowbridge Elementary then taught in the Detroit Public School system as teacher of Kindergarten to third grade, then as Reading Specialist in grades 1 through 6. Dorothy retired after thirty-five years as an educator.

———

John A. Henry lived with his parents; father Willie, mother Eula and two brothers, Robert and Charles at 708 Hendrie. John attended Balch Elementary, Garfield Intermediate and Northeastern High School. He also attended Wayne State University receiving a B.A. in Criminal Justice. At Atlanta University, John received a Masters in Criminal Justice. In 1948, John joined the U.S. Army and was a member of the 82nd Airborne Division at Fort Bragg N.C, aattaining the rank of Tech Sergeant and was honorably discharged in 1952.

In 1955, John joined the Detroit Police Department after a short stint of minor-league baseball with the Chicago Cubs affiliate in Janesville, Wisconsin. In the Detroit Police Department, he ascended through the ranks, attaining the position of Deputy Chief. In 1994, John was appointed Executive Director of the Police Athletic League where he served until September 1995. After retirement, John became very active at Bethel A.M. E. Church where he has been member for over 65 years and continues to volunteer his services to Bethel.

———

Robert L. Ellison (Deceased) born in Detroit to Zolie and Marion Ellison. Robert attended Balch Elementary and Garfield Intermediate schools. He graduated from Northeastern High School. Robert attended Wayne State University, earning a B.S.

Jr., Bertram and John at 5020 St. Antoine. Subsequently the family moved to 602 E. Warren (the present site of Plymouth United Church of Christ). 602 Warren was not only the family home degree in Pharmacy from the College of Pharmacy. Robert was an honor student for his entire academic life, even as he delivered the Detroit Times Newspapers in his neighborhood. As a child and as a youth, Robert attended Greater Bethlehem Temple Church.

While attending Wayne State, he was a starting guard on the nationally ranked basketball team for three seasons. At Wayne, Robert pledged Alpha Phi Alpha Fraternity. After graduating from Wayne, Robert matriculated at Meharry Medical School in Nashville, TN., earning his D.D.S. in 1960. Robert received advanced specialty education in Endondontics at the University of Pennsylvania Graduate School in Medicine in 1962-1965 and received a Master of Science degree from Temple University in 1965. Robert served in the U.S. Air Force at Castle Air Force Base in Merced, CA .as the Base Endodontist. Robert had one daughter, Cheryl Ellison Stack by his first wife, Marion.

———

Era June Irving Williamson, a native Detroiter, is one of seven children born to Lela and Sam Irving. She lived at 587 Medbury Street with her parents and siblings, Lillian, Joe, Wilbur, Gloria, Deloris and Dian. Era attended Balch Elementary, Sherrard Intermediate, Northeastern High School and later, Wayne University and Lewis Business College. After attending Wayne State, Era worked at the Ordinance Tank Automotive Command in Southwest Detroit. Era attended Mt. Olive Church and Bethel A.M.E. where she was a member of the Children's Choir and part of a group called "The Junior Housewives League. In the early 60's, Era moved to Philadelphia, PAA and attended Temple University. She owned and operated an Interior Decorating and Dress Design in Philadelphia. Era moved back "home" to Detroit in 1999.

———

Ernest Wagner Jr. is the older of two children born to Ernest and Annie Wagner. His longtime residence was at 676 E. Ferry where he attended Balch School. After graduating from Balch Elementary, he attended Garfield Intermediate and

Era June Irving Williamson

Ernest Wagner, Jr.

Northeastern High School. Ernest played baseball and basketball at Northeastern High School and was selected to the All-City and All-State basketball team. Although offered a scholarship to University of Michigan, Wagner chose to attend Wayne University. At Wayne State, Wagner was part of a unit that gave Wayne University the title "The First College Team in Michigan to play five African Americans. Wagner was recruited by professional basketball teams, but chose to play with The Harlem Globetrotter from 1954 to 1967. At present, Wagner works for the "Black Legends of Professional Basketball.

Justine Rogers Wylie

Justine Rogers Wylie is the third of four children of Luther and Lillie Rogers. Siblings were Marvin, Yvonne and Larry Rogers. A resident of the Near Eastside until adulthood, attended Lincoln Elementary, Garfield Elementary and Intermediate and Northeastern. After graduation from Northern High School, worked briefly for Michigan Bell Telephone, then left Detroit to attend and graduate from Howard University in Washington, D.C.

Returned to Detroit and became a Detroit Public School Teacher. She received a M.A. in Education from Wayne State University and taught at the Russell and Berry Elementary Schools.

Relocated to San Francisco, CA. and received a Master's Degree in Marriage and Family Counseling from San Francisco State University. Taught at San Francisco State for four years, then opened a therapeutic home, Cadence House, for children in crisis. Retired to Michigan to help care for an ageing parent.

Teola Cranon Hunter

Teola Cranon Hunter, a native Detroiter, was born on February 5, 1933 to T.P. and Olivia Crannon. She is the youngest of three sisters and one brother. She resided at 549 and 690 Med bury Street on Detroit's Near Eastside for most of her young life.

Teola attended Balch Elementary School, and Sherrard Intermediate School. She is a graduate of Cass Technical High School. She received her B.A. from the University of Detroit and her M.A. Degree in Educational Guidance from Wayne State

University. Teola was an active member of Bethel A.M.E. Church and was involved in several organizations. At Bethel, she was the first president of the Junior Housewives League. She also served on the Usher Board.

Jean Everage was born July 12, 1935 in Montgomery, Alabama to William and Julia Lena Everage. She had one sister, Bernice.

Bernice and Jean came to Detroit, Michigan in 1941, rejoining their parents who were already living in Detroit at 551 Medbury between Beaubien and St. Antoine. Jean relates, "My Mother, sister and I were members of St. Paul A.M.E. Zion Church at 521 E. Palmer near Beaubien St. I began school at Balch, 1st grade, September 1941, attended Sherrard Intermediate School, and graduated from Cass Technical High School."

Following High School graduation, Jean began working for American Telephone and Telegraph Company. Jean retired from Michigan Bell Telephone Company in 1989 after a career that spanned 36 years.

Jean Everage

Bessie Louise Williams Ernst was born on the east side of Detroit during the days of the depression Her parents were Walter and Bessie Lura Williams. Louise, as she was known by her classmates and Honey as she was called by her family was the eldest of eleven children

Bessie attended Balch Elementary, Garfield Intermediate and Northeastern High School. Bessie received a Bachelor of Arts Degree from Wayne University She received her Masters Degree from the University of Detroit. Bessie is an active member of Sacred Heart Catholic Church on Detroit's Near Eastside.

Bessie is the mother of four children, Steven, Janis, Michael and Linda. Her life's work has been primarily in education. Bessie credits some of her achievements as derived from her teachers at Garfield Intermediate School whose messages were "Don't look back, always look forward, for each generation must achieve and go further in education than their parent's generation. Be the best you can and don't be discouraged."

Bessie Louise Williams Ernst

186

John L. Kline, Ph. D.

John L. Kline was born and lived on Detroit's Near Eastside for most of his young life. John lived on Ferry Street with his mother, Rosabelle Colvard and his stepfather, James Colvard, 5 brothers and 1 sister. When his parents moved to St. Clair Street on Detroit's Eastside, John remained at the Ferry Street address with his Aunt and his Uncle Charley. He attended Balch Elementary, Garfield Intermediate and graduated from Northeastern High School in 1949, the elected president of his senior class. John attended Wayne State University on an athletic scholarship, where he was a standout basketball player, preparing him for the honors to come as a member of the famed Harlem Globetrotters. John received his Ph.D. in history and philosophy of education from Wayne State University.

Eugene (Geno) Elzy moved to Detroit as an infant with his parents, Eugene and Delfreda Elzy. Elzy lived in a two-family flat at Hancock and Beaubien before moving to 610 East Kirby where he resided for twenty-one years.

Eugene attended Balch Elementary, Garfield Intermediate and Northwestern High School. At Balch, he was encouraged to study music, mastering the clarinet and playing it throughout his learning years and in the All- City Bands. Elzy studied for eleven years at The Detroit Conservatory of Music along with Joe Hunter and James Jamerson of Funk Brothers fame. His exposure to jazz was the foundation of his future.

In the United States Air Force, Elzy was assigned disc jockey for the Armed Forces Radio at Ellison A.F.B. in Fairbanks Alaska. After he was honorably discharged, Elzy went to Professional Broadcasting School where Pierre Paulin and Jim Garret taught him the trade.

After working at radio stations WCHD and WCHB, Elzy joined radio station WJR as a staff announcer, becoming the first African-American Music Director at the station. Geno is known as one of the finest radio personalities in the city, hosting Black Journal. He treasures interviews he conducted with Muriel Humphrey. Lena Horne and Ossie Davis.

Eugene Elzy

Terry Louise Bagwell (Deceased) was born in Atlanta Georgia. She was one of three siblings including Sadie Bagwell Graham and John Bagwell born to Jessie and John Bagwell. Terry's educational background included Balch Elementary, Garfield Intermediate and Northern High School. Terry was a graduate of Morris Brown College with a B.A. in Social Work. She earned a Masters in Education from the University of Detroit with further studies at Atlanta University.

Terry has been employed as Police Officer for the City of Detroit, as Social Worker at Franklin Settlement and teacher at Field Elementary and the Stark School of Technology. Beyond these activities, Terry received a Masters Degree in Counseling and Special Education and a second Masters in Social Work.

Terry was a fervent churchgoer and a member of Sacred Heart Catholic Church for over 50 years. Terry was an active member and participant in many organizations including The Detroit Urban: League, JUGS, Inc., Alpha Kappa Alpha Sorority, Renaissance Lion's Club and the United Negro College Fund.

Herman Anderson, ESQ. was born in Detroit. He attended Sacred Heart School where a classmate remembers him as "the smartest boy in the class." Anderson graduated from Cass Technical High School. in Detroit. He lived on Ferry Street. Herman has been the legal consultant for the Near Eastside group.

Marjorie Shephard Davidson was born in Detroit to Millidge and Minnie Kate Shephard in Detroit. Marjorie lived with her parents and her only brother, Millidge Jr. on Medbury Street in a terrace

Terrie Louise Bagwell

Herman Anderson, ESQ

Marjorie Shephard Davidson

Alma Grace Stallworth

apartment. Marjorie attended Balch Elementary, Garfield Intermediate, and Cass Technical High School. She graduated from Eastern High School. Marjorie attended church sporadically, visiting the various neighborhood churches, Mt. Olive Baptist, St. Paul A.M.E. Zion and Bethel A.M.E. for her spiritual sustenance. Marjorie worked for the Detroit Municipal Credit Union after High School. Subsequently, she worked for General Motors and Electronic Data Systems in computer operations. Marjorie retired in 2003 and assumed the care of her brother, Millidge with whom she lives.

Alma Grace (Russell) Stallworth came Detroit with her family in 1938 Alma was one of four daughters that later became five when her mother divorced and later married Adolph Singley. Another sister, Deborah, was born to that union. Alma lived for many years on the corner of Warren Avenue and Russell, upstairs over the beauty salon owned by her mother, Lisbon. She attended Palmer

Elementary, Garfield Intermediate and graduated from Northeastern High School at age 15.

Because Alma's mother considered the neighborhood to be transient, she insisted that Alma spend her free time in church. The church was Bethel A.M.E., a central place or hub for religious and social activities.   When Alma joined Bethel, she blossomed! She was actively involved in the many programs sponsored by Bethel A.M.E. Alma's first employment was also at Bethel as an office clerk working with the late Madeline Wortham. She was responsible for recording dues, other contributions, memberships, baptisms, births and death records, publishing the Sunday School bulletin and the church newsletters. She served under two ministries, Reverend Alexander and Reverend Joseph Roberts.

189

Cyril Braithwaite and Olga Forde Braithwaite.

Chapter Twelve
Photo Gallery
of Near Eastside Families

The Braithwaite Family

The Braithwaite family originated in Port of Spain, Trinidad and the British West Indies. The patriarch of this family was Cyril (Cecil) Braithwaite, born in 1898 to Blanche and Donald Braithwaite. The matriarch of the family was Olga Forde Braithwaite born in 1904 to Juliet and Charles Forde. The couple met as children and grew up together. After serving in the British Army during the First World War, Cyril immigrated to the United States in 1919. Moving to Detroit, Cyril obtained employment at the Ford Rouge Foundry. Olga immigrated to New York in 1924 and married Cyril. The young couple's first home was on Frederick Street near Beaubien. To this union, four children were born, Cynthia, John, Sylvia and Cyril. They resided at 636 Hendrie and 632 Harper Streets.

Sylvia Braithwaite (1951).

(L to R) Sylvia (age 3), John (age 5) and Cynthia (age 9) Year - 1936.

John Braithwaite (Age 11).

Cyril Braithwaite, Jr., 1 year old (1941).

Sylvia Braithwaite, Holy Rosary.

Wedding of Cynthia Braithwaite and Leroy Howell (October 1950)
(L to R) Cyril, Jr., J. C. Hooker, Sylvester Urquahdt, Bride & Groom, Sylvia, and Olympia Barthelomew.
Reception at the Kappa House.

The Muthleb Family

Abdul Muthleb married Huldah Virginia Walton in Detroit, Michigan. Abdul Muthleb was born in Cheluva, District of Hoogly, India. Huldah Walton was born in New Iberia, Louisiana. They had five children: Three sons and two daughters. They were Ahmed, Joynal, Zebadah, Mildred and Abdul.

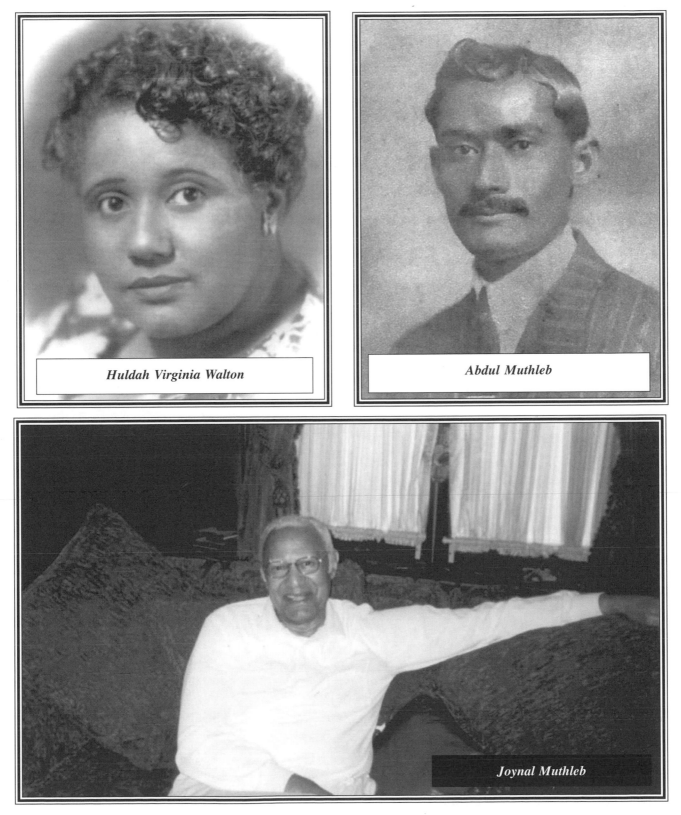

Huldah Virginia Walton

Abdul Muthleb

Joynal Muthleb

The Muthleb Children: (L to R) Ahmed, Joynal, Zebadah, Mildred and Abdul.
Taken at Lincoln Photo Studio, 5423 Hastings Street, Detroit, MI..

Cargle, Davis, Rowlette and Elzy Families

We may not have known the adage, "It takes a village to raise a child" but at 610/612 E Kirby, we certainly practiced it. Our village was a four family flat shared by the Cargle, Gibbs, Davis and Elzy families. Included in our village was the Rowlette family of Hendrie Street. Our village square was the second story porch where we would gather to talk, play and observe the village surroundings. From our village square, you could see Taxi's basement store, Scott Methodist Episcopal Church on Kirby and St. Antoine and all the homes along Kirby stretching to Hastings Street where Mike's Grocery Store was located. The families shared everything: wisdom, food, household equipment and gossip. During the Balch school years, Mrs. Elzy would prepare a delicious lunch for all of us. Many times, the girls would rush to finish eating so they could play a game of Jacks before returning to school. We formed a club called "The Funmakers" where we played many games as a family group. Bingo, Canasta and Monopoly were our favorites. We all attended Bethel A.M.E. Church where Rev. William H. Peck was the minister. Many of us became Bethel Sunbeams under the guidance of Priscilla Massey. After church, we would gather on our village square and watch the village happenings.

These were the wonderful fun times that we shared. It shaped and formed our friendships that have lasted over 50 years. Though each family moved away, we have never lost touch with each other, still sharing the trials and tribulations of life as we always did on Kirby Street.

Cheatham Thanksgiving Dinner, 655 East Kirby, 1946.
(L To R) Eugene Lester, Jr., Nancy Lester, Ina Webster, Oswald Webster, Alice Cargle, Rita Webster, Mame Cheatham, Albert Cheatham, Delfreda Elzy, Dianne Elzy, Veronica Webster, Ruperta Cargle, and Council Cargle.

Davis & Rowlette Sunday Dinner.

Coranell Rowlette, Eugene Elzy, Ilma Rowlette, Betty Rouse, & Florence Rowlette.

Alice Cargle

(Standing): Ruperta Cargle & Dianne Elzy. (Seated: Delfreda Elzy & Allison Cargle.

Charles Rowlette, Bruce Davis, Pearl Davis & Eddye Rowlette.

Council Cargle and mother, Alice Cargle.

The Elzy Family

Eugene and Dianne Elzy (Brother & Sister)

Delfreda Cathrin Webster-Elzy
(Mother)

Eugene Elzy, Jr. and his horn

Delfreda Webster-Elzy and
Daughter, Dianne Lenora.

Delfreda Webster-Elzy and son, Eugene
Ulery Elzy, Jr.

Terry Bagwell Family

Terry Bagwell lived an extraordinary life of service to humanity as a dedicated educator in the Detroit Public Schools, a volunteer, community activist, mentor, caregiver and humanitarian, but most of all, she was a devout Christian. She loved Sacred Heart Catholic Church, where she had been a member for almost 50 years, and of course, she loved Father Thomas (her godfather), who seemed to understand Terry and her persona. At Sacred Heart Church, she served religiously on the Pastoral Alliance and the Ministers Service.

Terry entered this world in Atlanta, Georgia on March 31, 1928, to bring joy to her parents, Jessie and John Bagwell. Her parents and siblings, Sadie and John, moved to Detroit, Michigan. Terry was educated in the Detroit Public Schools, attending Balch, Garfield and Northern High School. She was a graduate of Morris Brown College, where she earned her Bachelors of Social Work, a Masters of Education from the University of Detroit and further studies at Atlanta University. As an educator, she taught classes at the Stark School of Technology, the Moses Field, Bellevue and night classes at Northern High School. She also served as Student Teacher Director at Wayne State University. After 30

Terry Louise Bagwell
Sunrise: March 31, 1928 - Sunset: May 31, 2006.

years of outstanding service, Terry retired in 1994.

For those who knew Miss "T," as she was affectionately called, you know service was more than a word to her. She demonstrated her actions in feeding the homeless, collecting over 200 coats for the needy, helping students secure scholarships for Historical Black Colleges; camp supervisor and recruiter (money or no money - if they wanted to attend). While directing activities at the Franklin Wright Settlement, she sent many children to summer camp; providing clothing for the underprivileged, providing finance to bury six children who were in a house fire and of course, her annual Thanksgiving Feast for her friends where over 200 gathered to enjoy food, friends, and entertainment. Remember Nerfetiti - the only French Poodle to have annual birthday parties and a formal burial covered by the Michigan Chronicle - *that was Terry!*

198

Terry's Mother, Jessie Bagwell-Mumford

Terry's Father, John Bagwell, Sr.

John Bagwell, Jr. with Terry

Terry's sister, Sadie Graham

Erma and Alfred Zackery

The year was 1936 when Lottie White and her daughter Willie Earmie Robinson arrived in Detroit, Michigan from Springfield. Mass. They lived on Fredrick near St. Antoine. Willie enrolled at Garfield School. In 1937 she met Clinton Harris at a Valentine's party and later that year they eloped and got married in Chattanooga, Tenn. They returned to Detroit and in 1938 a daughter named Erma Lee arrived. They lived with Willie's mother Lottie on Hendrie and St. Antoine in the "Evelyn Pats". They remained at that location until 1950.

Erma attended Balch School on Palmer and St. Antoine thru fifth grade. During those early years Erma visited the cultural buildings and many movie theaters on a weekly basis, Main library and Art museum at Kirby and Woodward. The theaters were Warfield, Mayfair, Majestic, Roxy, Paradise and State.

At least once a month my mother would take me to the trolley to the Broadway market, where we would have a hot dog and Vernor's ginger ale treat.

In early 1937, Ralph and Effie Zackery left Atlanta, GA. They lived on Canfield near John R and remained in that area until 1950. Then both families moved from Near Eastside to the Northend of Detroit.

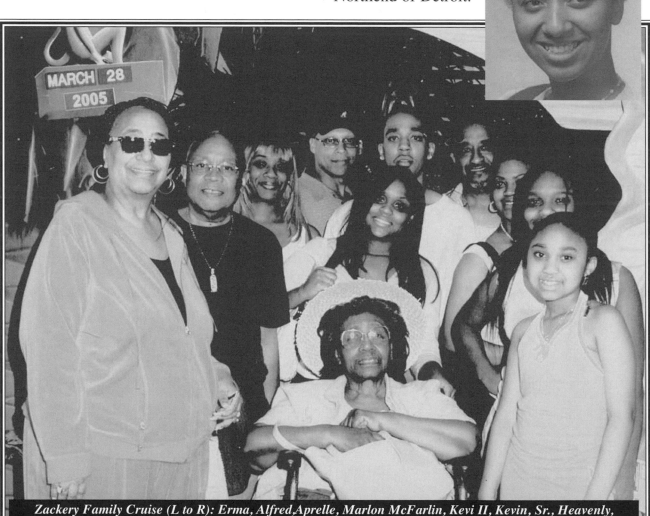

Zackery Family Cruise (L to R): Erma, Alfred, Aprelle, Marlon McFarlin, Kevi II, Kevin, Sr., Heavenly, Ashley, DeAdra, Brittany and Willie Earmie (Erma's mother, seated)
INSET: Erma Lee Harris (Graduation, 1956).

Erma lee Harris, age 5 (1943).

Alfred Zackery, 1939.

(L to R) Alfred Lamar Zackery, Ralph Zackery (father of Alfred & Michael) and Michael Zackery.

Kevin, Aprelle (R), Alfred & Erma Zackery family.

The Carter/Cranon Family

T. P. Cranon (Father) and Olivia Carter (Mother).

Samuel Carter (Brother)

Teola Cranon

Carter / Cranon Family
(Rear): Doris, Samuel & Teola. (Front): Julia bell, Andrea and Julia Lee.

The Johnson Family

The home of the Johnson family was located at 428 Eliot Street, a few houses down from St. Peter Claver School. Our parents were John Henry Johnson, Sr. and Mary Lizzie Johnson. They came to Detroit from Alabama in the 1920's. They had six children, Eartha Lee, Rose Marie, Doris, Georgina, John Henry Johnson, Jr. and Bernard Johnson. All six began schooling at Lincoln School on Brady.St. Though we were as poor as the next family, our family shared an open door, open arms, open pocketbook and open heart with who ever came to them in need.

———

Mary Lizzie Johnson (Mother).

Doris Johnson with her niece, Wanda, daughter of her sister, Eartha Lee.

John Henry Johnson, Sr. (Father).

Willie Aaron Williams Family

Willie Aaron Williams was born in Detroit to parents Hiram Williams and Leola Williams of Columbus, Georgia. He was the eighth of nine surviving sisters and brothers. He began his life in the 600 block of Superior Street, the same street inhabited by Mack Ivey, owner of the then famed "Black and Tan" Cozy Corner Night Club on Alexanderine and Hastings and inhabited also by other prominent blacks that included Dr. Stafford and his jeweler brother.

His siblings were Hosie, Ernest, Addie, James, Rena, Estella, Elizabeth and Mack, the youngest. Mr. Williams says, "We lived across the street from the Sophie Wright Settlement House, where my mother and many other blacks finished school and became proud citizens of the community and the city."

Mr. Williams began his education at St. Wenscelas Catholic School on St. Antoine and Leland. Later he attended Lincoln Elementary, Garfield Intermediate, and Northeastern High School from which he graduated in 1939. Later, he attended and graduated from Wayne University where he worked for Budd Automotive and attended classes. Mr. Williams was an accounting major.

At an employee at Budd Manufacturing, Mr. Williams became active in the UAW Local 306 and in the Credit Union at Budd. In time, he became Chairman of the UAW Credit Committee and later a loan officer. Subsequently, Mr. Williams left Budd and became a part of the International Credit Union. As a consequence of his experience with and knowledge of credit unions, he spent one year in Africa helping the people organize unions and credit unions.

Mr. Williams has been successful in his life and career. He says, "All of my success came out of the Near Eastside Neighborhood. Whatever I have gained in life, it all started in that Near Eastside community."

Hiram Williams (Father).

Willie A. Williams (on left).

Willie A. Williams

Mack Bernard Williams (Brother).

Mack Bernard (in front). Across table is brother, Hosie, and sister-in-law, Pauline Williams.

THE MITCHELL FAMILY
652 HENdRiE

Otey and Clara Mitchell came to Detroit, Michigan, from LeGrange, Ark., in 1929. Jewell Mitchell, their first born, was born in **Ark.,** she was two years old when they came to Detroit, Michigan. Mildred Mitchell, their second child was born in Detroit, Michigan, her mother was pregnant with her when she came to Detroit. Herman 0. Mitchell their third and last child, was born in Detroit, Michigan.

Otey Mitchell retired from Chevrolet Gear and Axle; he died in 1960. Clara Mitchell, a housewife and self taught beautician who also wrote poetry, died in 1970.

Jewell Mitchell retired from Chrysler. She had eleven children and many grand and great grand children. She was an excellent cook, and very talented in Arts and Crafts; she died in December, 2001.

Mildred Richardson retired from the City of Detroit in 1989; she was a counselor and Senior Counselor Aide for the City, She had three children, her son died in 1995; she has four grandchildren.

Herman O. Mitchell retired from the State of Michigan. He has two sons, one granddaughter and two great grand daughters. October 17, 1965, Herman O. Mitchell was a Bridge Design Engineer for the Michigan Department of Transportation. He did the layout and design of I-696 (east and west) over I-75, in Detroit Metro District and other bridges in the area. Herman is now a Tax preparer and Consultant.

————

Clara Mitchell, standing on right. Jewell Mitchell, standing on left. Herman and Mildred Mitchell on pony. Picture taken near Leader Drug Store, 1934.

207

Herman Mitchell and Delores Miller. Devera Lightsey is standing in rear. (1949, Bethel AME Church.)

Herman Mitchell and friend

Otey Mitchell, father of Jewell, Mildred and Herman, standing in rear of 422 E. Palmer, 1948.

The Greenfield / Hill Family

John Greenfield, Sr. and Naomi West Greenfield came to Detroit from Alabama in the early twenties. They met and married after Naomi West sought employmentand was hired as a secretary for the Eagle Moving Company, a busuness owned by John Greenfield. Four children were born to this union, Alfred, Jr., Bertran, Dorothy and John.

John & Naomi Greenfield
Eagle Moving Company

Dorothy Hill with Grandchildren. (L to R)
Daniel Hill, John Hill, III, Dagny Hill, Naomi-
Dianne Hill and Joshua Hill.

John & Dorothy Hill

John Hill, Dianne Hill, Dorothy Hill (Mother), David Hill and Steven Hill

209

(L to R Rear) Dr. David Hill,
Attorney Phylis Hill, Dagny,
and Dorothy Hill
(L to R, Front) little Naomi and
Great Grandmother, Naomi
Greenfield

John Greenfield, Naomi Greenfield and Dorothy
Greenfield Hill

The Edmonson Family

John Henry Edmonson, Sr. Was born in South Carolina. Georgia Ann McKieten Edmonson was born in Way Cross, Georgia. Mr. Edmonson was a contractor who travelled extensively for business. On one of his many trips, he met and married Georgia Ann McKieten. In the mid-twenties, after many moves, they settled on Detroit's Near Eastside and raised their eight children. All of their children have been successful in their professions and in their lives.

(From left bottom, clockwise) Georgia Ann, Lois Ruth, Florence Marie, Betty June, Ila Elisabeth, John Henry, Jr., Charles James, William Wesley, David Laurence and John Henry Edmonson, Sr..

William & Adrienne Edmonson

David & Virginia Edmonson

The John Henry and Georgia Ann Edmonson Family

Clarence & Lois Hepburn

Elisabeth & Charles Calloway

Mary & John Edmonson

Charles & Patricia Edmonson

Florence & Arthur Jackson

Betty & William Price

Millidge, Sr. (Patriarch)

Millidge Shephard, Sr. was born in 1906, in Eufala, Alabama. Minnie K. Scott was born in 1913 in Evergreen, Alabama. They both moved to Detroit during the late 1920's.

Minnie K. Scott Shephard (Matriarch)

The Shephard / Davidson Family

Erica

Eric, Dee, & Erica

Millidge, Jr. & Margie (Sister & Brother)

Isiah

Marge, II

Peter & Merle

Kia, Shaniece, & Tomasina

Peter & Makeisha

The Cooley Family-
Medbury Street

Reverend Paul Cooley, Sr. was born in Shawnee, Oklahoma and his wife, Mary Winslow Cooley, was born in Topeka, Kansas. In 1929, they and their 3 small children moved from Kansas City, Kansas to Detroit, Michigan. They lived on Division Street where my sisters, Gladys and Freida were born. Later, we moved to Pontiac, MI where Reverend Paul Cooley, Sr. became the pastor of "Church of God." My sister, Betty and brother, John, were born there

In the middle years of the 1940's, Mama and the children moved back to Detroit where we lived on Medbury Street. Mama's sister, Ruby Winslow, and their brother, Eddie Winslow, lived on Medbury Terrace, located on the northeast corner of Medbury at John R. Street.

Those were years of family togetherness especially with extended family in the neighborhood. The schools and churches along with other educational and memorable events filled our lives with many Blessed Memories. My parents and five of my siblings are deceased. My sister, Betty Cooley-Devereaux, now lives in Palmdale, California. I, Mary Cooley-Dendy, live in Los Angeles, California.

Rev. Paul Cooley, Sr.

Mrs. Mary Winslow Cooley

Freida Cooley-Wilkins

Paul Cooley, Jr.

Gladys Cooley-Nicholson

Marvin Cooley

Betty & Mary Cooley

John & Mary Cooley

Edward Winslow

214

The Claude B. Everage Family

Claude B. Everage came to Detroit during the 1920's. He was born in Montgomery, Alabama in 1904. After arriving in Detroit, he roomed throughout the area, now designated " The Near Eastside" living with family and friends. As a single working man, "rooming" was sometimes the normal and ideal lifestyle. He was a member of St. Paul A.M.E. Zion Church. 521.East Palmer near Beaubien.

Mr. Everage believed in working and was employed for many years with Federal Mogul Co. until the plant left Michigan. In our Dad's later years, he worked for and retired from the Ford Motor Comoany. He enjoyed the sport of wild game hunting with his buddies. Back in the day, he frequented the near-by clubs, restaurants, shoe shine stands and record shops on Hastings, St. Antoine and Brush Streets. He liked the old blues records, also enjoyed dressing well and driving his large Chrysler cars

He gave one of his teen-age nieces, Bernice Everage, her first driving lessons while driving to and from the popular Joe Louis Farms in Utica, Michigan. He was a very special uncle to his relatives and a wonderful helper to his friends.

As a single man in his middle 40's, he moved from the Near Eastside to the North End area, living near his sister, Mrs. Josephine M. Griffin. There he met and married a neighbor, Miss Dorothy Alston from Bluefield, West Virginia. They became the proud parents of four proud sons. Our parents are both now deceased.

We are: Claude Van Everage, William Griffin Everage (Deceased}, Curtis Burn Everage, and Clifford Eugene Everage.

Claude B. Everage and 4 sons,
Claude Van, Clifford, Curtis, and William Griffin Everage
(1964)

Claude B. Everage of St. Antoine & Medbury,
1946.. (From Montgomery, Alabama)

215

Miscellaneous

(L to R): Clara Norman, Ulysses Davis & Mamie Davis.

Mayor Coleman Young and Teola Cranon

Bernard Johnson Family
(L to R) Georgina Franklin, Byian Johnson, Doris Watlington and Marcus Johnson

216

EPILOGUE

Some say Detroit is fighting a losing battle to survive. Much of the housing is outworn. The factories have become obsolete and/or abandoned. Many of the best paying jobs in the automobile industry are gone. To a great extent, the middle class has moved to the northern suburbs. Property taxes are high, revenue is low, and the schools are poor despite the millions of dollars that come from the Michigan Lottery and the Casino taxes. Private investment has been slow.

Yet, there are many indications that Detroit is revitalizing itself. The cultural center of Detroit is intact and thriving. The DIA has completed a 158 million dollar renovation assuring its continuance as a premier art museum. Comerica Park, home to the Detroit Tigers, attracts hundreds of thousands to this city. The Hudson's Thanksgiving Parade, now Macy's continues to attract huge crowds to the city. The Red Wings, playing at The Joe Louis Arena in downtown Detroit, remain a key player in the NHL. The Detroit Lions have their very own Detroit venue in the beautiful new Ford Field on Detroit's Near Eastside. The casinos attract countless visitors to Detroit. That the casinos were able to build new and grand hotels is testimony to their continuing lure. Yet, ultimately, the heart of a city is its people and their faith in its continuance.

One Near Eastsider, **George D. Ramsey, Sr.** shares with you, his passion for and his memories of the city of his birth as he writes of **"Ole Dusty Detroit."**

I have been asked, " Why do you live in Detroit?"…My answer is simple. I choose to live in the city of my birth for many reasons. Most of all, because of the many fond memories I have of growing up in… Ole Dusty Detroit.

These streets are where I learned to ride a bike and roller skate, where I delivered the Detroit Times from my old rickety wagon and rode with the iceman in his horse drawn wagon. I've enjoyed sun filled mornings, afternoon picnics in city parks and love filled evenings on Belle Isle after dark in Ole Dusty Detroit.

I have worn America's pride of Joe Louis on my sleeve. During World War 11, Detroit's sweat and labor made this city the arsenal of defense. I've marveled that my town was in the forefront of social activism. Labor unions that became the catalyst for social change throughout the world started right her in Ole Dusty Detroit.

I have seen Superbowls and Superstars at Ford Field, "mega events" and dancing gents kicking high at the Fox Theater on Woodward Avenue. I have cruised the Detroit River while watching the fireworks lighting the cities sky, and enjoyed the international flavor of Canada on the front doorstep of…Ole Dusty Detroit.

For some it may never be the city that it was during the 40's and the 50's, but for me it always will, because as long as I remain here, so will those glorious days because of my memories of…"Ole Dusty Detroit. "

Justine Wylie
Editor-in-Chief

Bibliography

The Detroit Almanac, 300 years of life in the Motor City, Edited by Peter Gavrilovich and Bill McGraw, The Detroit Free Press, 2000.

Detroit in its World Setting: A Three Hundred Year Chronology. 1701-2001. Edited by David M. Poremba. Wayne State University Press, Detroit, 2001

C. Eric Lincoln and Lawrence H. Mamiya, *The Black Church in the African American Experience.* Duke University Press, 1990.

Ernest H. Borden, *Detroit's Paradise Valley.* Arcadia Publishing, 2003.

Loren D. Estleman, *Jitterbug,* Tom Doherty Associates, Inc., Publisher, New York, N.Y., 1998

Berry Gordy, *To Be Loved, An Autobiography,* Publisher Warner Books, Inc., New York, N.Y. 1994

Wilbur Rich, *Coleman Young and Detroit Politics,* by Wayne State University Press, Detroit, Michigan, 1989.

Della Reese, *Angels Along the Way,* Published by G. P. Putnam's Sons, New York, New York, 1997

Mary Wilson, *Dream Girl, My Life As A Supreme*, Published by St. Martin's Press, New York, 1986

Hillary Rodham Clinton, *It Takes A Village,* Simon & Schuster, 1996, New York, New York

www.History.com

Michigan Citizen

Detroit Free Press

Michigan Chronicle

Heritage House Museum